The Secret Life of a Cultural Diplomat

Paul Woods

DEDICATION

This book is dedicated to my wife Fanta who has followed
me faithfully around the world from 1981 onwards, and to
all my former British Council colleagues and the many
friends whom I met on the way.

CONTENTS

ACKNOWLEDGEMENTS

Acknowledgements are due to all those sources quoted in the bibliography, including the often anonymous authors of files downloaded from the internet.

1 THE PHILIPPINES

I emerged from university with a degree in Russian and History. This was 1971, the year that Britain kicked out 105 Russian spies. So all of a sudden the bottom dropped out of the market for Russian linguists, unless you wanted to either teach Russian in one of the relatively few secondary schools where it was being taught as a foreign language, or carry on at university doing research and then become an academic. (I had contemplated doing a PhD on Khomyakov, an obscure 19th century Russian religious thinker). Or you could join GCHQ and become a spy.

I really wasn't sure what I wanted to spend my working life doing, but then a year spent teaching English as a British volunteer working for Voluntary Service Overseas in the remote North-East State of Nigeria convinced me that what I really wanted to do was to work for the British Council. I had seen the overseas arm of the Council in action at relatively close quarters and I fancied the lifestyle of an expatriate overseas, but with the security provided by a permanent pensionable post, the kudos and excitement of a semi-diplomatic lifestyle, and the responsibilities of a managerial role rather than direct teaching in the classroom.

I knew it was highly competitive, with around 3000 initial applicants a year for fewer than 30 places. To my great surprise I got through the preliminary interview and was invited to a "group selection board". I must have given too many wrong answers, because at the feedback session following the board the verdict was, "We think you're a bit young and immature, Mr Woods, but you do have potential. We suggest you go off and do something else for a few years, then if you're still interested, re-apply."

So that's what I did. I put in for a range of teaching jobs overseas and got interviewed by British Aircraft Corporation to teach English in Saudi Arabia on their long-running military aircraft project which preceded the controversial British Aerospace Al-Yamamah arms deal. At the interview at Wharton Aerodrome near Preston, I was asked what other jobs I was applying for. Perhaps naively, I revealed that I had also applied for teaching jobs with The British Council (teaching English in Mongolia) and The Crown Agents (as an Education Officer in Brunei). The interviewer then spent the next ten minutes telling me why either of these would be more interesting than working for BAC!

So I spent the next three years helping to run a primary English project for the government of Brunei, then the following ten years on a series of two-year contracts funded by the Overseas Development Administration, managed by The British Council, training primary school teachers of English in Tanzania and Sierra Leone.

By 1987 my third two-year contract in Sierra Leone was coming to an end, and the prospects for further relatively lucrative aid-funded posts in English Language teaching looked fairly slim, as ODA was starting to have doubts about the value of English as a tool for development. This was the start of the decade when academics such as Phillipson, the author of "Linguistic Imperialism"[1] questioned the role of English and aid agencies soon followed suit. Encouraged by my wife, Fanta, I decided to have a final go at joining the British Council's Overseas Career Service (OCS) before I became too old. A year or so prior to the end of my contract in Sierra Leone, in July 1986, I sent off an application to join the OCS. This was before the days of rapid e-mail communication and a letter via the diplomatic bag used to take several weeks or longer to reach its destination. After about a month I received an acknowledgement of my application. I then went off on two months annual leave to the UK, expecting to hear something further before returning to Sierra Leone at the beginning of September, and hopefully to take advantage of being back in the UK if called to attend an interview.

However, there was only silence. By the end of October I complained to the Council Representative in Freetown, George Reid, that the very least they could have done would be to send me a formal note that my application had been rejected. George promised to follow it up, and a few weeks later a minute arrived from the Overseas Educational Appointments Department saying, "We don't usually lose people's application forms but we appear to have lost his," and advising me to re-apply. This meant that when I did finally get invited for an interview followed by a selection board I had to pay my own airfare. Whether this demonstrated such amazing keenness that it influenced the outcome I never discovered. Following the group selection board I was told that I had been invited to a final selection panel with six members of the great and good. I don't recall much about it, apart from someone asking, "We see this is the second time you are applying to join the British Council, the first time being 15 years ago. Do you notice anything which has changed with our selection procedures in the interim?" The only thing I could think of to say was, "Well, as far as I can recall, last time in the psychological test there was a question asking 'Do you suffer from diarrhoea at great heights', but this time round it had changed to "Do you suffer from constipation at great heights?" To my great surprise, I got a letter a few days later saying I was being offered a post and initially would be working in the Technical Cooperation Training Department in Spring Gardens, just round the corner from Trafalgar Square.

In an article for Foreign Policy[2], Mark Leonard outlined the four purposes for public diplomacy in the twenty-first century:

- increasing familiarity – making people think about your country and updating their image of it
- increasing appreciation – creating positive perceptions of your country and getting others to see issues from your perspective
- engaging people – encouraging people to see your country as an attractive destination for tourism and study and encouraging them to buy its products and subscribe to its values

- influencing people's behaviour – getting companies to invest, encouraging public support for your country's positions, and convincing politicians to turn to it as an ally.

In the early 90s the Council's focus was still on 5 main areas of activity – English, Science, the Arts, Education and Exchanges, and these cultural relations goals had not yet been clearly articulated.

So in July 1987 we packed up and said our farewells to all our friends and contacts in Sierra Leone and rented a flat in Watford from where it was a relatively easy commute to Euston then down the Northern Line to Charing Cross.

My first day in the Technical Cooperation Training Department (or TCTD, as it was known) was something of a disaster. I was to work as a programme officer, responsible for the files of around 70 trainees who were studying in the UK, mostly for one-year masters degrees, and shadowing the person responsible for the China desk, running the Sino-British Friendship Scholarship Scheme. The head of section gave me the files for two Burmese students, Tan Bin Tee and Tin Bee Tan and a great sheaf of papers, instructing me to file these away in the correct file for each student. When she came back a couple of hours later to check what I had done, she said, "You're going to have to do a lot better than this, Mr Woods. You've got half of these papers in the wrong person's file."

My stay in TCTD was relatively short. After a few weeks I was told that from early in the new year I was being posted to The Philippines as the Assistant Representative. This was a fairly small office in the British Council scheme of things, and it would be treated as a training post, which would allow me to both use my ELT professional skills (they had previously had a full time English Language Officer, Graham Millington, but had just abolished his post) whilst at the same time I would be supervising work in the Arts, Exchanges, and Finance. The Representative, Hugh Salmon, was a former colonial civil servant in Uganda who had subsequently joined the Council and was now on his final posting before retirement. The Council office was located in a splendid old Spanish colonial-style building hidden away in a back street in New Manila, one of the smarter suburbs of metropolitan Manila. This still had the original wooden floors and traditional opaque capiz shell windows in each office. Unlike modern-day open-plan Council offices, everyone had their own room, apart from a couple of local staff who shared an office. The ground floor was a large well-stocked library ably managed by Cora Monroy. We were to take over the lease from my predecessor on a smart two-storey villa with a swimming pool, located in a walled village just a stone's throw from Greenhills shopping centre, and only ten minutes' drive away from the office on a good day. On the odd occasion when the traffic lights failed it could take an hour and a half or longer. Our last few weeks in the UK were spent in a flurry of preparations, including buying various household goods considered necessary for the representational role I was about to take up. The Council had an arrangement with John Lewis, so most of our shopping was done there. Back in the 1980s, Council staff in "representational" grades were given a generous monthly entertainment allowance to be spent on taking key contacts out for meals or for providing cocktail parties and dinners for visiting experts and local VIPs. If you didn't spend your annual allowance in full it was a black mark against you! So we needed sets of plates and cutlery, glasses and other items for hosting dinners and cocktail parties. In order to qualify for a loan to buy a car you had to buy British, so rather than ship a new car out from the UK we arranged to buy my predecessor's second hand Rover saloon. Not a problem until one day it rolled backwards down the driveway, across the road and into a wall, needing a new back bumper which had to be shipped out from the U.K. at vast expense.

This was the first overseas country apart from Sierra Leone where we had lived since getting married. It was fine for me, but Fanta as a black African found it could be something of a strain at times. The first time we went to the nearest beach, a two hour drive to the south of Manila, where we walked along the water's edge, I was conscious that every eye was following us like spectators on the centre court at Wimbledon. Although many Filipinos are quite dark skinned, the only Africans they ever saw were US servicemen from the huge Clark air force base north of Manila at Angeles City. When Fanta told someone she came from Guinea the usual reaction was, "Ah, New Guinea!" She had to explain that she was from Guinea in West Africa rather than somewhere to the north of Australia.

Not long after we arrived in Manila, we set off one Saturday to look for some large round table tops which could be placed on top of the smaller square tables provided by the British Council so that we could sit ten or twelve people round the same tables when we were entertaining. We found some in a Chinese-owned store downtown, but as they were much too large to fit in our car we agreed with the shop owner that Fanta would come back with a British Council driver to pay for and collect them early the following week. When she went back to the store the following Monday there was a different person behind the counter. She explained what she had come for and presented him with the cheque I had given her, only to be told, "We don't accept cheques from negroes." Storming out in a rage, Fanta retorted, "Well, you can keep your bloody tables – I'll get them somewhere else!" Such incidents were not uncommon and made it difficult at times for Fanta to feel at home in Manila. A few days afterwards we were invited to a Chinese restaurant for dinner by one of the Council's ELT contacts. At some point during the evening Fanta, assuming the other guests were all Filipinos, began telling this story, and when she ended with a fiery condemnation of Chinese racism, the host tapped her on the shoulder in a friendly sort of way and said, "Fanta, you do realise, don't you, we are all Chinese here?"

When I returned to The Philippines three decades later to check out the prospects for employing Filipino teachers on an innovative project to teach English remotely in Uruguay using videoconferencing, I gave an interview to Isagani Cruz, an old friend who wrote regularly for the Philippine Star. Cruz wrote, "Woods was the Assistant Director for the British Council in the Philippines from January 1988 to September 1991. When I asked him what he remembered best about those years, these are the things he listed: The Arts programme we ran in Intramuros; one of the highlights was a one-man show by an actor who played Houdini and escaped from a straightjacket and tanks of water onstage. Visiting places like Cagayan de Oro to run workshops on English for Specific Purposes. The send-off party for Lea Salonga, who was leaving for London to star in Miss Saigon. The time when Salman Rushdie's Satanic Verses was published and a protestor set a copy on fire inside the British Council library. Staying one time in a completely empty 300-room hotel in Ilocos Norte. Visiting the Malacañang Palace when it was opened to the public for the first time. The time when there was an attempted coup against President Aquino and we were holed up in Greenhills East for several days before the action moved to Makati."[3]

The Council's Arts programme in the Philippines was ably managed by Vikky Magsalin. She used to attend all the Arts events we were involved with, often in the evenings, and so used to clock up huge amounts of time off in lieu for working overtime accompanying performers we were sponsoring or attending events organized by our partners and collaborators. Every so often we had to pay her off, rather than giving her the time off, or we wouldn't have seen her for weeks at a stretch.

The one man show based on the life of Houdini was part of a two-month long tour of South-East Asia organized centrally by the Council's Arts Department. We had an arrangement with the administration of Intramuros, the old walled city in downtown Manila which included the original Spanish fort, under which we regularly provided British performers for open-air theatre and concert performances within the walls, and also sponsored groups of Filipino actors and musicians to put on plays and music by British authors and composers.

The actor was arriving from somewhere in the South Pacific, via Australia, and when he arrived at Manila airport it was clear he was absolutely exhausted from the hectic schedule he had followed over the previous few weeks. The show was extremely physically demanding, involving escaping from a strait-jacket whilst tied upside down to a gallows, and from a tank of water he was submerged in and locked into, amongst other things. We reluctantly cancelled the first couple of performances, but the actor assured us he would be fine after a couple of days' rest, so we lined up a local band at short notice as a front act, just in case, to avoid any further cancellations. In the end the show was a huge success.

Looking after the Arts brought me into contact with the great and good of the Philippines arts scene. One of the staunchest supporters of the British Council was Naty Crame-Rogers, who with her husband Col. Joe, a Philippine Air Force pilot, frequently attended Council-supported events. An institution in Philippine theatre, Crame-Rogers had been an actress, director, producer, author and drama teacher, living by the mantra 'Life is drama, drama is life.' According to a recent article in The Inquirer, "She established the Philippine Drama Company Sala Theatre 32 years ago under the principle that... "dramatists can use their own homes as a workplace, a tradition among Asian artists, by converting any open space such as the sala into a stage." Crame-Rogers believes that if people find going to the theatre hard for various reasons such as traffic or busy schedules, then why not bring theatre to their homes? She is her own example: except when she got ill, she's been using the sala or living room of her home in Pasig City as a performance venue. Her immediate family members, nephews, nieces, neighbours and students rotate roles as actors, backstage crew and audience. When her husband Joe was still alive, he either acted in her plays or served as part of the backstage crew. A common scenario in Sala Theatre productions is the audience becoming part of the show; a major aim of "seducing" people into such a setup is to help them "become better individuals after experiencing theatre," said Crame-Rogers."[4]

Other excellent partners were Zenaida Amador, the Founder and Artistic Director of Repertory Philippines, and Maria Teresa Roxas, the first President of the Cultural Centre of the Philippines in the post-Marcos era.

One of the highlights of our stay was when Cameron Macintosh came to Manila looking for performers to star in a new musical, "Miss Saigon." A child actor and teen idol, Lea Salonga, was selected for the role of Kim. According to Wikipedia, "Unable to find a strong enough East Asian actress/singer in the United Kingdom, the producers scoured many countries looking for the lead. For her audition, the then 17-year-old Salonga chose to sing Boublil and Claude-Michel Schönberg's "On My Own" from *Les Misérables* and was later asked to sing "Sun and Moon", impressing the audition panel. She competed for the role with childhood friend and fellow Repertory Philippines performer Monique Wilson. Salonga won the lead role, while Wilson was named her understudy and given the role of the bar girl Mimi. In 1999, she was invited back to London to close the West End production."[5] Before the two performers set off for London, there was a rousing send-off party which we were involved in.

A significant part of my responsibilities was to support English language teaching. Graham Millington had been the full-time English Language Officer until his post was suppressed, and one of the challenges was to keep all the English Language Teaching balls in the air. We had a project in Ilo-ilo in the Visayan islands to support the development of English for Fisheries, funded by the Overseas Development Administration. This was ably managed by our Key English Language Teaching Officer, Mike Smith, who worked very closely with his Filipina counterpart, Eunice Torres. They were attached to the Iloilo State College of Fisheries, and one of the outcomes of their project was a textbook on "English for Fisheries Technology."[6] The Fisheries Project had close links with the University of Lancaster's English department. I used to lie awake at night worrying that Mike regularly had to travel all round the country with Eunice and they might end up getting attached romantically. However, my fears proved completely groundless: Eunice later went off to Lancaster for further studies and ended up falling for and getting married to Tom Hutchinson, one of her lecturers at Lancaster and a prolific author of English language textbooks.

One of the tasks which fell to me as Assistant Representative was to accompany visiting "Spectourists" (so called because the department in the UK which made arrangements for their flights and contracts was called Specialist Tours) to the more dubious nightspots of Manila, which were concentrated in the area around Ermita, basically acting as a sort of "minder". During the first term of Mayor Alfredo Lim in the early 90s, an effort was made to clean up Ermita's image and reputation. A local city ordinance prohibiting the establishment of motels, lodging houses and other similar establishments was later declared unconstitutional by the Supreme Court, but only after the red light district had moved down the coast a bit towards Malate.

One of the weirder establishments in Ermita was the Hobbit House, started by Jim Turner, an ex-Peace Corps volunteer, who was associated with it until his death in 2016, after which it closed down. Given the accolade by Lonely Planet of "one of the world's most trippiest bars", most of the waiters and other staff in the Hobbit House were dwarves. At first the whole thing felt "blush, exploitative, wrong, degrading."[7]

However, according to the Washington Post, "The Hobbit House ... soon became a haven for the dwarves Turner rescued from the capital's streets and from carnivals and variety shows that demeaned them. He employed dwarves as waiters, bartenders, cashiers, entertainers, even bouncers. Eventually, they became managers and owners. Over the years, children and grandchildren of the original staff found employment at the Hobbit, one of the few places in the Philippines where dwarves could earn a decent living and not be shunned as outcasts, or even feared as the embodiments of evil spirits."[8]

English for Specific Purposes (ESP) was being widely promoted in the 70s and 80s by the British Council and ODA, and I welcomed the opportunity to visit some of the more remote parts of the country delivering talks and workshops on ESP-related topics. One of the many interesting locations I visited was Loag, in Ilocos Norte, which had been a major stronghold of support for

President Ferdinand Marcos, who had recently been replaced by Corazon Aquino. "The Marcos Mansion or Bahay Ti Ili was the birthplace of President Marcos. The province where the mansion is located is famous for grand ancestral homes, and this is one of several grand homes owned by the family. The great mansion showcases family memorabilia, especially mementos of Marcos' military service during World War II, his political career, and his 20 years of presidency. There is a display of family photographs and portraits, some 33 life-sized statues of Marcos dressed in a variety of outfits, his car license plates from his years as a congressman, and letters that he wrote addressing the Filipinos during his exile in Hawaii."[9] The organisers of the visit booked me in to the magnificent Fort Ilocandia Resort Hotel, with over 300 rooms, where I seemed to be the sole guest for the entire duration of my stay! During the Marcos years I imagine the hotel would have been very popular, but with the demise of the Marcos regime it had fallen on seriously hard times!

Graham Millington had managed to establish excellent relationships with a very wide range of institutions and I was fortunate to be able to pick up where he had left off. Amongst our ELT contacts were representatives of all the major institutions involved in ELT in Manila, including Brother Andrew Gonzalez and Tish Bautista at De La Salle University, Edna Manlapaz and Malu Vilches at Ateneo de Manila University, Gemino Abad at the University of the Philippines, Gloria Chan at the Asian Institute of Management and Casilda Luzares, who subsequently moved to Japan. Brother Andrew later went on to become Secretary of the Department of Education,

Culture and Sports under the presidency of Joseph Estrada. He had a brother who owned a restaurant which served the most delicious soufflés imaginable.

The publication of Salman Rushdie's *Satanic Verses* in September 1988 caused some excitement. Kenan Malik wrote in the Observer,[10] "Rushdie was then perhaps the most celebrated British novelist of his generation. His new novel, five years in the making, had been expected to set the world alight, though not quite in the way that it did...Within a month, *The Satanic Verses* had been banned in Rushdie's native India. By the end of the year, protesters had burned a copy of the novel on the streets of Bolton. Then, on Valentine's Day 1989, came the event that transformed the controversy – Ayatollah Khomeini's fatwa calling for Rushdie's death. The fatwa forced Rushdie into hiding for a decade. Bookshops were firebombed... The controversy over *The Satanic Verses* brought into focus issues that have since become defining problems of the age – the nature of Islam, the meaning of multiculturalism, the boundaries of tolerance in a liberal society and the limits of free speech in a plural world. That, 30 years on, we still blindly wrestle with these issues reveals how little we have learned from the Rushdie affair. And how the lessons we have learned have often been the wrong ones." In Manila a protestor managed to gather together a pile of papers in the centre of the British Council library and set them alight underneath a copy of Satanic Verses before he was forcibly removed by security guards.

Concerned about the threat from Muslim and other activists, and shortly after a grenade had been thrown through the windows of the United States Information

Service library in the central business district of Makati, as well as a bomb going off at the USIS library in Davao, we were advised by the Embassy security officer to install a metal detector at the entrance to the British Council. The guards on the gate had strict instructions that civilians and military were to leave their weapons at the entrance along with any other suspicious-looking metal objects. Not long afterwards there was a bit of a panic when the guard on the gate phoned through to the Representative's secretary to say that someone was heading up the stairs to Hugh Salmon's office with something metal in his backpack. The alarm was sounded, the bomb squad summoned and the building hurriedly cleared of staff and visitors. It turned out that the backpack contained a cake tin, within which was a cake brought as a gift for the Representative by a returned study fellow as token of gratitude.

One of the most interesting places to visit in Manila was the Malacañang palace. When President Marcos was overthrown in the 1986 People Power Revolution, the palace complex was stormed by protesters who roamed the grounds. The main palace was opened to the public not long after we arrived in Manila and was converted into a museum for the next three years. Amongst the items on display was Imelda's famous collection of over 8,000 pairs of shoes which had been left behind in her wardrobe when the president and his wife fled. Imelda was later quoted as saying: "They went into my closets looking for skeletons, but thank God, all they found were shoes, beautiful shoes." Thirty years later, hundreds of pairs of the first lady's shoes can be found on display at the Shoe Museum in the northern Luzon city of Marikina.

The Philippines is a stronghold of Catholicism, with around 85 per cent of the population being practising Catholics. There is also a substantial and at times vocal Muslim minority in the south, especially in Mindanao. Protestants make up around 6% of the population, with charismatic and Pentecostal mega churches using mass media techniques experiencing particularly rapid growth. On Sundays we attended the English-speaking Greenhills Christian Fellowship just down the road in the nearby shopping mall, and often followed the service with dim sum at a nearby Chinese restaurant. GCF had begun in a small way when Rev. David and Patty Jo Yount of the Conservative Baptist Mission felt called to work with emerging, self-reliant Filipinos who had the influence and the leadership skills to do a significant work in spreading the gospel. It began on February 14, 1978 when 67 people met at the Club Filipino for a Valentine's Fellowship Dinner. GCF grew and eventually settled in to rented premises on the second floor of the Medecor Building along Ortigas Avenue later in 1978. Not long before we left Manila, in 1990, GCF had laid the foundations for its own purpose-built church building at the corner of Garnet and Ruby roads in the Ortigas Center, Pasig City.[11] When I revisited Manila 30 years later I discovered it had outgrown the "new" building, moved into even bigger premises on the lot next door, and now had around 8000 members.

Various tests had shown that Fanta would need a minor operation if she got pregnant in order to avoid losing the baby. Naturally we were both delighted when in mid-1990 she discovered she was pregnant. We checked with several doctors on the Embassy panel in Manila about having the procedure done locally, but they all seemed rather vague about it. The advice from the FCO medical scheme in London was that she should go to Singapore or Hong Kong to have the operation carried out at about 12-16 weeks. With hindsight I should have taken some leave and accompanied her, but the British Council in Hong Kong assured us that they would send a Council driver to meet her at the airport and take her to the hospital which was half way up the peak on Hong Kong Island, and then arrange for her to be taken back to the airport when she was discharged from the hospital. The Chinese driver duly collected her as planned but on arriving at the hospital gate said that was as far as he was going, so heavily pregnant and at risk of losing the baby, she had to lug a large suitcase several hundred yards up a steep hill to the hospital entrance. Fortunately all went well and she arrived back safely in Manila armed with a bottle of pills to stop her going into labour prematurely if she needed to fly anywhere.

The next couple of months passed uneventfully, but at the beginning of December all hell broke loose in Manila. Between 1986 when Corazon Aquino became President and the end of 1987, there had been six plots to oust her, involving various disaffected factions including members of the Reform the Armed Forces Movement (RAM) and loyalist supporters of former president Ferdinand Marcos, who had been deposed in the "People Power Revolution" in late February 1986. Two of these coup attempts, the November 1986 "God Save the Queen" plot and the July 1987 plot, were discovered by the authorities before they were put into effect. The other plots were repelled with relatively little violence, the most serious being the

August 1987 coup attempt, which left 53 dead.

The most serious coup attempt of all broke out on Friday December 1, 1989, led by members of the Armed Forces of the Philippines belonging to the Reform the Armed Forces Movement (RAM) and soldiers loyal to former President Ferdinand Marcos. We were both at home when early in the morning we saw an ancient Tora Tora World War II vintage biplane circling around over in the direction of the presidential palace, then dropping what appeared to be a bomb, which exploded with a loud bang. This was followed by several jets flying overhead at close to the speed of sound. We later discovered that rebels had seized Villamor Airbase, Fort Bonifacio, Sangley Airbase, Mactan Airbase in Cebu, and parts of Camp Aguinaldo. The rebels surrounded the airport runway at Manila International Airport and launched planes and helicopters which bombarded and strafed the Malacañang Palace, Camp Crame and Camp Aguinaldo. It was quite difficult to find out exactly what was going on. As the Embassy's "warden" for the Greenhills area, I was responsible for liaising with any British subjects within the area in the event of a mass evacuation, but meanwhile the advice from the Embassy was to stay indoors and lie low. Camp Crame, the police HQ, and Camp Aguinaldo, the army HQ, were only about half a mile away on either side of EDSA, the arterial road linking the north and south of Manila. According to Wikipedia, "Three hours after the fall of Villamor Air Base, Aquino went on air to address her people, and declared that "We shall smash this naked attempt once more." At that point the government counter-attack began. Seven army trucks headed for Channel 4, and fierce fighting occurred there."[12] President Aquino requested military assistance from the U.S. and marines from Subic Naval Base were sent to defend the US Embassy compound on Roxas Boulevard. The Americans helped to clear the skies of rebel aircraft, thus allowing Aquino loyalists to consolidate their forces. While many mutineers surrendered, Aquino declared: "We leave them two choices; surrender or die." Government F-5 jets flew sorties against the rebel planes, destroying the ancient rebel Tora-Toras.

For the next two days everything went quiet. We felt quite safe, as we could see there was a contingent of government troops stationed in the supermarket car park down the road a couple of hundred metres to the west, and there were also government troops based in Camp Aguinaldo about half a mile to the north-east. However, after a couple more days the troops in the supermarket car park began tearing off the government insignia from their sleeves and it looked as if they might be changing sides. Our Austrian neighbours who worked for the UN told us that the UN had made a block booking for their staff at a hotel downtown in Makati, the central business district, and that we were welcome to join them. We vacillated for a bit, then eventually decided that we couldn't take Wellington, our Doberman, to the hotel, and as our maids had disappeared at the first signs of any shooting there would be nobody left in the house to look after him. So we decided it would be best to stay put. Fierce fighting continued throughout the weekend, with Camp Aguinaldo set ablaze by rebel howitzers. On the morning of the third day, loud gunfire could be heard just outside the walls of our village. It sounded as if there was shooting in the back garden, although it was actually a couple of blocks away. There was still sporadic shooting around noon, and I decided the safest place to eat lunch was in the bathroom, which had no windows exposed to the street or to the garden at the rear. However, Fanta said she certainly wasn't going to eat her food in a toilet, so she stayed out in the living room which had a large picture window overlooking the swimming pool. We debated whether she ought to take the pills she had been given in Hong Kong to stop her going into labour.

In the afternoon the government announced on the radio that the coup had been crushed. Government forces recaptured all the military bases except Mactan Airbase by December 3rd, but rebel forces retreating from Fort Bonifacio then occupied over twenty high-rise buildings along Ayala Boulevard in the business area of Makati, including the hotel where our UN neighbours had taken refuge. They even managed to shoot a hole in the bullet-proof glass of the visa section of the British Embassy. Our neighbours and the other hotel guests took refuge in the hotel's basement car park where they were forced to huddle together in pretty grim conditions for several days. We were very grateful to Wellington for having saved us from the same fate.

We were already planning to return to the U.K. for Christmas and had booked our flights well in advance. The Representative Hugh Salmon and his wife Helena were still holed up in their walled village near Makati, but we were able to contact them by phone and Hugh agreed that if the airport was open and it was safe to drive there by a roundabout route avoiding Makati, we should set off as planned. We felt a bit guilty going off and leaving them to an uncertain fate, but as it turned out the occupation of Makati ended a couple of days later, on December 7th, while the rebels surrendered Mactan Airbase on December 9th. The official casualty toll was 99 dead (including 50 civilians) and 570 wounded.

Fanta was advised to stay on in the U.K. with my brother Ian and his wife Julie for the next four months until she had the baby. The fact that Ian worked as a GP meant he could keep an eye on her and facilitate arrangements for the delivery, which was planned for towards the end of April. Meanwhile I went back to Manila to pick up where I had left off. Shortly afterwards Hugh and Helena left and a new Representative, Norman Bissett, took over, accompanied by his wife Faith.

The British Council agreed that I could take two weeks' leave in April, so I was back in Liverpool in good time for the safe arrival of James Jawara McClure Woods at Fazakerly hospital on 26th April. Shortly afterwards I had to return to Manila, with the intention that we would get James a passport and Fanta and the baby would fly back a couple of weeks later. The flight was booked, but there was no sign of James's passport arriving. So Fanta set off without it. I anticipated all kinds of problems with the immigration authorities in Manila, but she just sailed through passport control with no questions asked.

Our final few months in Manila passed very quickly. I learned that I was being sent on a "direct transfer" from Manila to Brazil, to take up the newly created post of English Language Officer. The British Council hadn't decided whether to locate the post in Brasilia or Rio, so we made arrangements to ship our heavy baggage, not quite knowing where to send it to. It finally turned up in

Brasilia nine months later. The Council recruited a successor, Lesley Hayman, to replace me as Assistant Representative, but then in a masterpiece of undiplomatic bungling informed her just a few weeks after she had arrived in Manila that they were abolishing her post.

2 BRAZIL

The journey to Brazil with a six-month-old baby was quite an undertaking, involving a long-haul flight across the Pacific to Los Angeles, where we spent a couple of nights before catching the onward flight to Rio, then another short flight the next day from Rio to Brasilia. Until it had been agreed where my post was to be located, we were to stay in the centrally-located Hotel Nacional for a few weeks – though this turned out to be several months. James seemed to have difficulty adjusting to the new time zone: the difference between Manila and Brasilia was exactly 12 hours, so midday in Brasilia was midnight in Manila. For several weeks he seemed to spend most of the night wide awake and most of the day sleeping soundly.

The British Council office was about ten minutes' drive away off Via W3 Norte in a somewhat run-down area of Brasilia surrounded by motor mechanics and petty traders. The office was vertically stacked up on five floors, with an information centre on the ground floor, and the Science and Forestry departments on the top floors. English and Exchanges were somewhere in the middle.

This configuration was quite bad for a sense of corporate identity, as you only ever went up to the top floors on rare occasions and only really interacted closely with staff working on the same floor. Brasilia was one of those new capitals which were created from nothing at an arbitrary site in the sixties and seventies, like Canberra in Australia, Abuja in Nigeria and Dodoma in Tanzania. It was founded in 1960 to serve as the new national capital and has now become Brazil's third most populous city. Planned and developed by town planner Lúcio Costa and architect Oscar Niemeyer, the idea was to move the capital from Rio de Janeiro to a more central location roughly equidistant from all corners of Brazil. The basic city plan is like an aeroplane, with the presidential palace on an east-west axis located where the pilot sits, government ministries and public buildings located in the area of the fuselage where the first and economy class cabins would be, and two wings Asa Norte (north wing) and Asa Sul (south wing) stretching out on either side, with residential areas, organized into "quadras" (blocks) off the main arterial roads. The north wing is a mirror image of the south wing, and we once drove around 15 miles to an address in Asa Norte, only to find that we should have been at the same address but thirty miles away in Asa Sul. The two wings were designed to contain 96 "superquadras" with buildings limited to six stories high and 12 additional superquadras limited to three-storey buildings. Costa's intention with the superquadras was to have small self-contained and self-sufficient neighbourhoods and uniform buildings with apartments of two or three different categories, where the upper and middle classes would share the same residential areas.[13]

According to the BBC, "By common consent his buildings for Brasilia are elegant and astonishing. 'Hauntingly beautiful' and 'absolutely magical' is how the British architect Norman Foster describes some of Niemeyer's buildings in Brasilia. 'A great body of work by a great architect. There's a wonderful optimism and beauty and light about them. They make life richer for everybody who uses them,' says Lord Foster. He calls Niemeyer's presidential palace, in particular, a gem."[13] The problem with Brasilia is that it is not a city which has grown organically. Modern urban planners champion mixed use neighbourhoods. However, in Brasilia, on the other hand, everything was to be zoned. "It's got a place where you go to work. There are places where ambassadors have to sleep, and they are extremely unhappy about that because there isn't any street life," says Burdett.[14] The apartment building complexes that the left-leaning Niemeyer designed to house the rich and the poor are now home to the rich and the rich, while the poor – drivers, maids, shop assistants and security guards – live half an hour's bus ride away in satellite cities which often resemble a shanty town, with piles of rubbish in the streets and unmade roads, which turn into a quagmire when it rains heavily. Not unlike apartheid South Africa. It's problematic being a pedestrian in Brasilia; the roads are not designed for pedestrians and similar shops are often concentrated in the same quadra, so if you need a fridge you head for a quadra where all the shops selling electrical goods are located, for a pharmacy to the quadra with pharmacies and for a book to the one with bookshops. Ahead of the presidential palace in the pilot's seat is a large lake, and on the far side of the lake residential areas have been built. We were fortunate to find a nice two-storey house to rent, largely built of wood, with a swimming pool and a pleasant garden, located in QI8 Conjunto 2, not far from the Gilberto Salomao shopping centre and across the Pte das Garcas bridge. The Council insisted we install a fence round the pool, as a small child belonging to one of the Embassy staff had tragically drowned in a swimming pool not long before. We got a loan from the British Council for a new car and also bought a cheap second-hand car, so we had one each. Elsewhere this would have been a luxury, but in Brasilia it was a necessity. People living in Brasilia appreciate Niemeyer's work but the city can be tough to live in. "It's difficult as a pedestrian. It doesn't always feel like it's on a scale designed for humans," says Lucy Jordan, a journalist in Brasilia. "The poor have been shunted out to satellite cities, which range from proper well-built cities to something more like a shanty town. So the utopian ideal hasn't exactly worked out with Brasilia."[15]

Over 75 million people of African descent live in Brazil, giving it the second largest black and mixed race population in the world after Nigeria. The census in Brazil distinguishes 5 categories, with percentages for each in 2010 as follows: brancos (white) 47%, pardos (mixed race) 43%, pretos (black) 7%, amarelos (Asian) 1% and indigenous 0.5%. On average, salaries for whites are 46% higher than blacks, so although racism is not overt, there is nevertheless an underlying element of this combined with social class differences based around income. But it was much easier for Fanta to blend in than it had been in The Philippines.

As English Language Officer, my diplomatic skills

were tested to the limit. We had four offices in Brazil, Sao Paulo, where the Council Director John Tod was also Director of the Cultura Inglesa and the Assistant Director, Terry Toney, an experienced ELT professional, was Academic Director; Rio, where one very experienced ELT expert Mike Potter had just been replaced by another, Tony Deyes, as Council Director; Brasilia, where Ray Newberry, another ELT person, was now nearing retirement, and Recife in the North East, led by Simon Cole. Each of these had their own budgets and priorities, and my task was to coordinate everyone's efforts in English teaching with only a relatively small budget at my disposal.

The Council had a long-established but somewhat ambivalent relationship with the Culturas Inglesas. The old-established Culturas in Rio, Sao Paulo, Belo Horizonte and Curitiba, amongst others, were multi-million pound enterprises and were generally foundations overseen by a Board of Directors. Rio and Sao Paulo between them had over 100,000 students and numerous branches. There were also newer Culturas which were often family businesses or had a single owner/director. One of the USPs which distinguished Culturas from other private language schools, of which there were many, was that they were the recognised centres in Brazil for University of Cambridge (UCLES) English examinations. This was a monopoly which the Culturas had guarded jealously, ever since the first three candidates from Culturas had passed the Cambridge Proficiency in English exam in December 1940. Other major players were commercial language school chains like Berlitz and Fisk, and Brazilian-owned franchise schools with names like Pink and Blue Freedom and Follow Me, where the English language was promoted and packaged like McDonalds Chicken Nuggets. There was even one chain of schools named Wizard which used to advertise on the sides of buses, "Wizard – Learn English in 24 hours". This turned out to be 24 hourly lessons on their beginners' course rather than a single magical course lasting for just a day.

Shortly before my arrival in Brazil around a dozen other British-oriented language schools which were competitors for the Culturas, and generally co-existed in the same towns, including the Independent British Institute (IBI) in Brasilia, led by Sara Walker, and Britannia in Rio, under Susan Mace, came together to set up LAURELS, the Latin American Union of Recognised English Language Schools. Some Cultura Directors uncharitably pointed out that they were recognised only by themselves.

In 1988 UCLES had swallowed up the Royal Society of Arts (RSA) examinations board, and the challenge was to give everyone a fair bite of the cake. The Culturas were deeply unhappy that the RSA exams had now de facto become UCLES exams, threatening their monopoly. There were about ten RSA/UCLES exam centres in five different countries in Latin America. Relations between the Culturas, UCLES and the British Council in Brazil were strengthened by the signing of a joint UCLES /ABCI/British Council examinations management plan in the early 90s. At the same time, a compromise was reached under which, although LAURELS schools could run the RSA exams, only Culturas could run the "main suite" of UCLES exams (PET, KET, FCE, CAE and Proficiency). The British Council retained its monopoly on the remittance of exam fees from Brazil to UCLES, taking a percentage to cover its administration costs. This was a niggling irritant to the exam centres, who did not feel they got anything much in return for the Council taking its cut. In fact, the new arrangement seemed to keep everybody in a nicely-tempered state of discontent.

Another source of irritation for the Culturas, which I had to manage, was the relationship with the Culturas and the British Council in the north-east. I got off on a good footing with Culturas soon after we arrived in Brazil when the Council Director Ray Newberry agreed that Fanta and I could spend a couple of weeks either in Belo Horizonte or Fortaleza studying Portuguese at the local Cultura. Having checked the map, we opted for Fortaleza, mainly because it had a reputation for beautiful beaches. This was fully deserved. We had a great time, studying for several hours each morning, doing our homework on the beach in the afternoons and dancing the night away to the sound of forro and lambada in one of the many nightclubs dotted around the beach area in the evenings. And we did manage to improve our Portuguese!

Shortly before my arrival, the Council Director in Recife, Dr Simon Cole, in an effort to expand his operation, had set up a British Council-run language school on the Council's premises. This was seen by the Cultura Directors in the north east, many of whom were related to each other and to the "godfather" of north east Culturas Israel Gueiros, who ran the Cultura in Maceio, as unfair competition, and possibly the thin edge of a very large wedge if the Council in its wisdom were to decide to set up its own Teaching Centres in Brazil. The Recife Centre was quite an innovative affair, with perhaps a little too much power in the hands of the teachers, who had introduced what they called the "retrospective syllabus", where teachers and students agreed what they would study in each lesson or series of lessons, and the teacher had to conjure up suitable lesson plans and materials accordingly, then record the lesson plans retrospectively. Carried to extremes, this put a huge burden on the teachers, who had to be able to find suitable teaching materials at the drop of a hat. Give them their due, they managed to build up an impressive bank of materials to draw on, classified and filed away for every conceivable point of grammar, vocabulary, syntax and style. The appointment of Eddie Edmundson, who until then had been the Director of Studies within the centre, as the "English Language Trainer Adviser" brought some semblance of order to the curriculum and syllabus, and it was agreed that he would spend a significant proportion of his time on training activity directed towards the needs of the Culturas in the north east of Brazil.[16] At the same time, the Culturas were reassured by an informal agreement that the Council's courses in Recife would be restricted to study skills courses for people intending to study overseas. This meant there were never likely to be more than a couple of hundred students at any one time, compared with the 8000 students studying a wide range of courses, including a large number taking courses for young learners, at the various branches of the Recife Cultura.

After a couple of years in Brazil I had gained the confidence of the Cultura Directors sufficiently to be given responsibility for carrying out inspections of existing and new Culturas to ensure that they came up to the expected standards. This meant that over the course of my four years in Brazil I was able to visit around forty of the sixty or so Culturas or aspiring Culturas then in the country. I described one of these visits for *Concord*, the Journal of the English Speaking Union:

"Flavio Serique Filho lives in the remote Amazonian township of Santarem. He speaks English fluently, with an accent which sounds vaguely Liverpudlian. Those who meet him for the first time are astonished to learn that he is entirely self-taught. In the 1960s, whilst playing in a band, he laboriously transcribed thousands of pop songs from English into Brazilian Portuguese, and later perfected his English by working as a tourist guide. In spite of his accent, until three years ago, Flavio had never been further afield than Belem at the mouth of the Amazon. Several years ago he set up his own English Language school, "Quick 'n Easy", with 300 students and one teacher. Through sheer hard work and persistence he built the school up to the point where he enjoys the strong support of the British Council, which sponsored his attendance at a teacher training course in the UK and has collaborated with Flavio to stage multimedia exhibitions on British Film Stars and The Beatles. He is now on the verge of joining the Brazilian Association of Culturas Inglesas. Flavio's story illustrates the extraordinary degree of interest in learning English which never ceases to astound first-time visitors to Latin America."[17]

I had to tactfully point out to Flavio that, were he to apply to join ABCI, amongst other things, students would have to buy original copies of textbooks, rather than using photocopies. The highlight of my visit was a trip down the Amazon to a remote beach not far from "Fordlandia", a rubber plantation project set up to supply Henry Ford's factories in Detroit, where we picnicked and admired the scenery.

Sadly, Flavio passed away a few years later in 2002, but will always be remembered as a larger than life character. Following his untimely death, the school was renamed Escola de Ingles Prof. Flavio Serique in his honour.[18]

Other fascinating visits included one to a would-be Cultura in Cacoal, in the state of Rondonia, near the border with Bolivia, deep in the Amazon jungle. This was a ten-hour bus ride from Porto Velho, along a road which follows the line of the old telegraph for about 1000km from Porto Velho to Cuiaba. Here the wife of the doctor at the local hospital had set up a small language school and had aspirations for it to become a Cultura, an ambition which she achieved shortly afterwards in 1995. Various indigenous tribes inhabit the border areas of Rondonia and the population of the state has grown dramatically over the past 70 years from around 70,000 to over half a million.

In Manaus I visited another language school, founded by Paul Hardy from Guyana and his wife Elsa in 1990, which had recently applied to become a Cultura. It now has three branches in Manaus and Boa Vista. The highlights of my stay were a visit to the Opera House, opened in 1897 at the height of the rubber boom in Brazil, with its under floor ventilation system and electric light, which was a rarity in the Amazon at that time, a night-time river trip dodging crocodiles, and being hugged round the neck by a giant sloth. At the mouth of the Amazon in Belem is another opera house, opened in 1878 and built in a Greek classical style. The Cultura Inglesa here was founded in 1993 and is another success story, with nine branches now dotted around the city.

In an article published in the LABCI News,[19] I argued that the concept of synergy (defined by the OED as "increased effectiveness or achievement produced as a result of combined action or cooperation") could be applied to the relationship between the British Council and the Culturas in Brazil. In 1993 for the first time the Council had supplied all the Culturas with a set of reference materials which they could use to answer queries about studying in Britain, acting as a first point of call. To help the Culturas stay one step ahead of their competitors, we implemented a joint project to set up "open learning" resource centres in sixteen Culturas, with the Culturas providing over £500,000 in capital expenditure and on-going funding of £175,000 p.a., and the Council providing consultancy expertise (through Eurocentres), seminars and basic resource materials. 90% of the participating Culturas said they would recommend others to set up their own self-access centres. Phase 2 of this project, from 1994 to 1996, set up state-of-the-art Computer-Assisted Language Learning/Multimedia centres in the same Culturas.

Cultura sponsorship of the Arts was one of Brazil's big success stories, with the Council identifying suitable shows and managing the overall tour, and Culturas acting as local venues and co-presenters for events. One of the events I helped to organise was a tour of Brazil by actors with the BBC English Roadshow, who visited nine cities giving seventeen performances of two plays, *Muzzy Goes on Holiday* and *The Seven Deadly Sins*, over the course of three weeks. Other joint activities included summer schools in the UK and Brazil, courses in management for senior Culturas staff and even courses for front desk and secretarial staff in marketing and customer service skills. Working with the state sector, the Council set up six English Resource and Information Centres in north-east Brazil and a further four in UNESP campuses and at the Federal University of Bahia in Salvador.

From time to time I used to visit Rio, where the Council invariably booked all but VIP visitors into the modest Debret Hotel, overlooking Copacabana Beach, which curves for 4km round the bay. Copacabana, along with Ipanema beach (immortalised in the song "The Girl from Ipanema") is famous for beautiful girls wearing the skimpiest of skimpy bikinis (known locally as "fio dental", or "dental floss"). The beach can be quite dangerous, however, with a high risk of being mugged. We were advised to take nothing with us when going to the beach apart from swimming trunks, a towel and flip flops, to leave any expensive watches and jewellery behind locked in the hotel safe, and only to carry enough cash for any immediate needs. Otherwise, and especially at night, it was best to jump into a taxi immediately upon leaving the hotel. On one occasion we had a group of sixteen agents from the UK visiting Rio and Sao Paulo for an Education Fair, taking place in Rio at the legendary Copacabana Palace hotel. Despite being warned of the risks of muggings, nine out of the sixteen managed to get themselves mugged during their week-long stay in the country.

I have never yet managed to succeed as a poet or novelist, but I did get into print in the LABCI News with

a poem inspired by the sight of some abandoned roses
spotted in the sand as I was taking an early morning walk
along Copacabana beach.

> There they lay,
> still wrapped in paper,
> five red roses
> stuffed in the sand.
> Not far away,
> an empty bottle of champagne.
> How did they get there,
> those five red roses?
> Had two lovers
> sated with passion
> stumbled off forgetting
> the symbol of their love?
> Or a young man,
> waiting for the girl who never came
> drunk and abandoned
> his thwarted hopes in tears?
> Or had a street child,
> tired of importuning
> planted the roses
> in the vain hope
> they might grow
> to a better future?
> I ambled on
> and when I returned
> they were gone.

Tony Deyes, the Director in Rio, had a flat to die for –
five or six storeys up, right on the seafront at Ipanema,

with fantastic views overlooking the beach. However, even paradise is not without its problems. The nightlife in Rio goes on well into the small hours and the flat turned out to be so noisy that when the lease was up they moved to a much quieter flat several blocks away from the seafront.

One never really felt threatened with being mugged in Brasilia, though this could lead to a false sense of security. On one occasion I was laying the trail for the weekly Hash House Harriers run in Brasilia with a girl who worked at the British Embassy. This involved a couple of "hares" marking a trail with shredded paper and chalk, which the runners then followed for several miles, and which stopped every few hundred yards at a "check" to allow the slower runners to catch up. Perhaps inadvisably, we had chosen a route which took us across Brasilia's equivalent of Manila's "Smokey Mountain" – a large area of wasteland where all the city's rubbish was dumped. We were heading across the dump leaving a trail of paper for the runners when we spotted a very dubious-looking character coming towards us. My co-hare said she didn't like the look of him, but I brushed this off. When he got up close he waved a gun around and demanded that I hand over my watch and wedding ring, plus another expensive sapphire ring which Fanta had bought for me in Bangkok. It was early December. "Come off it, it's Christmas," I argued, at which the hand holding the gun began to shake visibly and he threatened to blow my foot off if I didn't cooperate. Must be drunk or high on drugs, I thought. Deciding that compliance was my best bet, I handed over my watch and the rings.

Seeing my plight, my fellow hare had hidden her

valuables in her knickers, so all he got from her was a bag full of shredded paper and a box of chalk. He then ran off. We carried on laying the trail with some few bits of remaining chalk and a plastic bag of shredded paper, and only after the run was over did I go to the nearest police station to report the theft. I told the police I thought it was a toy gun, but when I described it in some detail they said, "Oh, no, that was a 22 calibre revolver. You did the right thing to hand everything over and not try to put up any resistance." That was how I acquired my Hash nickname – "Victim."

You cannot stay for four years in Brazil and not take part in Carnival, which takes place each year in February. The parade is the core of the Brazilian Carnival we know today. There are two major types of parades in Brazil: the more traditional ones, organized by samba schools; and "Carnaval de Rua" (street carnival), which are more informal parties in which people gather on the streets to the sound of "trios elétricos", trucks with loudspeakers blasting out very loud live music.

The first year, not long after our arrival, we stayed in Brasilia and were really quite disappointed. So the following year we decided to do things in style and see the Carnival in Rio, where the main event takes place in a specially designed stadium called the Sambodromo. Here the schools are judged on their elaborate floats, costumes, dancing and music. This is a very important competition and some samba schools spend over four million dollars on outfits and preparations.[20]

It is possible to rent a costume and join in the parade in Rio – my colleague Christine Melia did this – but with a small baby we preferred to just watch. Fanta had brought some ear plugs for James as we were near the front row very close to the drummers and the constant noise was deafening.

The following year we went to Recife in the northeast, where the main event takes place in the streets of the old town of Olinda. "Carnival in Olinda is mostly free (unless you pay to go to the private parties) and is made up of open-air parties that play *frevo,* a typical genre from Brazil's northeast that is fast-paced and animated. Olinda's Carnival is centred on folk traditions, so rather than the large samba parades, huge figurines are paraded throughout the town representing saints and spirits, known as *mamulengos*. One of the most famous of these huge dolls is the 10-foot tall *Homem da Meia Noite* (Midnight Man) who is carried through the streets at midnight to symbolize the beginning of Carnival. Olinda is all about the street parties which take place across the city. The street parties (known as *blocos*) are large crowds of people that follow a slow-moving truck that meanders through the streets blasting out music. The first official Carnival street party is *Sábado de Zé Pereira* which starts on Saturday and begins with a huge parade of street puppets and live music, and is represented by a large rooster figurine on the city's bridge. It attracts a crowd of about two million people, but there are plenty of smaller parties constantly going on throughout the next few days that are less intense, in terms of crowd numbers. [21]

Another highlight was visiting Foz Do Iguaçu. My parents, who by now were quite old, came out to Brazil and joined us for this trip. We splashed out and stayed in the only hotel within the boundaries of the Iguaçu national park, the five star Hotel Cataratas (which currently charges £350 per night for a room). The hotel had traditional Portuguese-style rooms, with dark wood panelling and furniture and the restaurant provided magnificent views over the falls. From 7 a.m. to 9 a.m. the trails overlooking the falls are exclusively for hotel guests. James enjoyed pushing his pushchair up and down the trails till he was totally exhausted.

Brasilia was an ideal place to have a small child. On Sundays we would usually attend the English service at the Union Church, then take James to one of the many playgrounds in parks around the city. A favourite spot was a churrascaria which also had a children's playground in the Parque da Cidade. James became quite fluent in Portuguese after he starting going to a play group/kindergarten near to where we lived. One time when I went to pick him up the children were dancing and long after the music had stopped James refused to let go of his partner and carried on whirling her around the dance floor.

When Ray Newberry retired, Patrick Early arrived in Brasilia, accompanied by his wife Stephanie. Patrick worked very hard on learning the language and was soon extremely fluent, to the point where he could give impromptu speeches in Portuguese. I managed to get on the wrong side of him when early on I turned down an entertainment claim for dinner for Patrick himself, Stephanie and their Portuguese teacher which included steak and a couple of bottles of wine. Going strictly by the book, 70% of the guests at any official entertainment should have been Brazilian to qualify for it being charged to the entertainment allowance. Patrick managed to upset Honor Flanagan, the Assistant Director, who was living in a house owned by the Council over the road from the Director's house, by cooking up a plan with the Global Estates department to convert the Director's house into the office and informing Honor that they were going to move into her house and she would have to find a smaller house or flat to rent.

A few months before we were due to leave Brasilia our daughter Marie was born in September 1994 at a private hospital in Brasilia. Everything went smoothly and we were delighted to now have both a son and a daughter. I applied for various overseas posts but nothing suitable came up and I learned that I would be posted to the Consultancy Group in Manchester as a 'Consultant in Language and Development'. This would mean quite a big drop in income, as I would no longer get various overseas allowances. But it was a chance to live in our own house in Chester for the first time, to get one's face known at headquarters, and to mingle with the great and good of the Council's English teaching cadre.

CHAPTER 3 CONSULTANCY GROUP

In the early 1990s the British Council, in a cost saving effort, moved about half its headquarters staff from London to Manchester. The site of Gaythorn Gasworks, teeming with toxic chemicals, was cleaned up and redeveloped by British Gas in a £27 million project known as 'Grand Island' and chosen by the Council from amongst 240 potential sites all over the country. The Council moved into a newly-built grey-tiled building adorned with many works of art, an impressive six storey high atrium with a magnificent 100 metre square carpet, and a rather interesting 25 metre high clock based on a sundial, with two revolving semicircles which created a golden sun at mid-day and a black semicircle at midnight. Any savings were more apparent than real, as staff who were previously employed in London but did not want to sell up and buy a house in Manchester were given a generous relocation package including "detached duty", which meant the Council paid their rent for the duration of their stay up north whilst they could rent out their house in London for a much higher rent than they had to pay in Manchester.

The first day of business at this new Medlock Street location was 16th March 1992. The purpose-built office included a restaurant to seat up to 150 people at a time, a bar which had Wilson's bitter on draught, and a crèche for up to thirty children from six months to five years old. The Council was to occupy this building for the next five years until a further round of cuts in 1997 led to downsizing and a move to smaller, cheaper premises in Whitworth Street.

The ELT section of Consultancy Group to which I had been assigned occupied a corner of the third floor and from my desk I could spend the afternoons daydreaming, gazing out at the trains passing over the carefully renovated railway viaduct arches which housed artefacts from the gasworks which had previously occupied the site. These were early days for computers at work and one staff member recalled, "I was having trouble with the disk drive on my pc, reported it to the IT help desk and got a copy of a message describing the problem, "customer has dick stuck in drive!"

There were 200 staff in Consultancy Group, including ten ELT consultants and I was assigned to a small sub-team of two, working under Richard Webber on Language for Development. The job was quite a challenge, as DFID under Clare Short was in the process of pulling the plug on aid-funded English language teaching. "Language for Development" was no longer "sexy", and the trendy new fad in the British Council was "English 2000". Nobody quite knew exactly what this was, but with the millennium fast approaching it was a catchy title. Various UK institutions tried to stem the tide ebbing away from language for development, including Lancaster

University, which organised the LAP 2000 Conference in 1992, but to no avail. Funds for English teaching were switched from aid to developing countries to the 'Know-How Fund', aimed at keeping the newly-liberated satellites of Russia in Eastern Europe onside. These were almost without exception keen to develop ties with the West and to join the EU and NATO. Voices like that of Antonieta Celani, the doyen of English for Specific Purposes in Brazil, whose "frequent defence of the role of the English language as the principal medium of international communication and the belief that one can only promote the value of a country's contributions that benefit mankind as a whole, by ensuring that these reach the widest possible audience worldwide through a language that has global currency,"[22] increasingly became voices crying in the wilderness as far as the developing countries of the third world were concerned.

We had bought a house in Chester back in 1985 but had never lived in it for any length of time. With hindsight we should have moved in and stayed there for the duration of my posting to Manchester, but we thought at the time it would be best to rent it out and find somewhere closer to Manchester to live. We rented a house in Sale and having tried unsuccessfully to get James into our first choice of primary school, settled for the nearby Woodheys Primary School. After we got burgled and when the tenancy on our house in Chester was due to expire, we decided to move back there and I would drive to work in Manchester each day. This worked out really well, as James was able to start school at Overleigh St Mary's, just across the field behind our house.

One of my tasks was to manage the Hornby Trust's funds, overseeing the selection of scholars to study in the U.K. and allocating funding for seminars for teachers overseas. Another was to help organise the annual "Dunford House" seminar, by then no longer held at Dunford House in Sussex, but at Alston Hall in rural Lancashire. I acted as Seminar Director for the 1995 seminar, on "Language Skills in National Curriculum Development", which brought together participants from thirty different countries with a very wide range of interests within the overall area of language skills and curriculum development. As I said in the preface to the seminar report, "We were able to draw extensively on recent British experience with the National Curriculum in English, Modern Foreign Languages and English as an Additional Language, with presentations by representatives of the SCAA, OFSTED, LEAs and university Departments of Education."[23]

I was also responsible for managing the UK end of the UK Immersion Project for Student Teachers from Hong Kong (UKIPST) and for monitoring the success of summer courses at various UK universities held under this programme. This involved a marathon three-week road trip round the country in August and September 1995, accompanied by an attractive young Chinese lecturer, Tse Tso Yuk Wah, who was representing the client, the Hong Kong Institute of Education. We spent several days in each venue, starting off at the Institute for English Language Education (IELE) in Lancaster, then taking in the Centre for English Language Teacher Education (CELTE) in Warwick, Chichester Institute of Higher Education, the College of St Mark and St John in

Plymouth, South Devon College in Torquay, and finishing up with Christ Church College in Canterbury.

Our overall conclusions were that:

"there was general agreement amongst all the participants that the courses provided them with invaluable exposure to the British way of life, through their homestays, taught courses and visits, had made them more confident in using English and had developed their oral fluency. Some students felt the courses had paid relatively little attention to reading and writing, or had neglected teaching methodology. However, as all of these could be done equally effectively in Hong Kong it seems sensible that the programme should continue to focus primarily on those areas (such as oral fluency) which can most effectively be tackled within the context of an immersion programme."

Some of the comments are quite amusing. One teacher "appeared to have lost the respect of the group by her behaviour the previous week, teaching without shoes on, and cadging a cigarette off a student teacher in the no smoking area of a restaurant during a visit".[24] In Torquay some students mentioned their fear of pets, as well as having to walk long distances late at night to reach their accommodation.

Yuk Wah's subsequent 1997 evaluation of UKIPST was very positive, indicating:

"The immediate effect of UKIPST is that participants gain tremendous confidence in speaking English. They overcome the psychological barrier of fear of making mistakes in speaking ...UKIPST forced them to think in English without mental translation from Cantonese to English before speaking. Such training, though for six weeks only, has a long lasting effect. They become more ready to speak in English after UKIPST... Exposure to a different culture, living with a host family, visiting different cultural and educational places and studying in a foreign country...have had great impact on the participants' personal growth and widening of horizons."[25]

From time to time there were opportunities for me to do short consultancy visits overseas. At times I felt like a jack of all ELT trades but master of none, as I didn't always have the background and experience to speak with an authoritative voice on the projects or proposals which I was advising on or evaluating, though the Council did send me on several crash courses, including one on proposal writing. I managed to bluff my way through.

In July 1995 I carried out a consultancy in Uzbekistan with Gill Sturtridge of Reading University, looking into the English Language Needs of the World Bank's Aral Sea programme. The Aral Sea, once the fourth largest lake in the world, had by 1995 shrunk by more than half its surface area, with dire social and economic consequences for the five countries in Central Asia which depended on water from the Syr Darya and Amu Darya rivers. The Know How Fund had agreed to provide funding for one of the sub projects – Hydrometeorological Services. We were to carry out a needs analysis, looking at the language and communication needs of personnel involved in the project, identify sources and costs for general and specific ELT courses, assess resource requirements and training needs for local teachers and put forward low cost options for improvement. There was no pre-arranged programme and I remember sitting over breakfast in the hotel in Tashkent with Gill on the Sunday morning after an Uzbek Airlines flight which arrived around 3.00 a.m., wondering just exactly how we were going to get started and who we ought to ask to see. Martin Seviour, who was working as a teacher trainer at the University of World Economics and Diplomacy, whom I had known as a VSO in Sierra Leone, proved very helpful in steering us in the right direction and putting a programme together, with further help from Janusc Kindler, a World Bank consultant working on a different sub-project. However, it all came together and over the course of a week we were able to meet with a full range of Glavgidromet staff, potential ELT providers, including staff from the Universities of World Languages and World Economics and Diplomacy, various World Bank staff and consultants and on our return to the UK produced a report setting out a range of costed options, including a teaching and self-access facility within the Glavgidromet complex, a two year project with a long term adviser/trainer post or a mixture of short term consultancy and a UK-recruited teacher. Other options we looked at included setting up a centre within the University of World Languages at Chorchu, and computer-mediated distance learning via a virtual classroom linking learners in all five Aral Sea republics.

Later that year I was part of a team of three including Andy Thomas, the Regional English Coordinator and Sue Buckwell the Regional Information Coordinator, both based in Lagos, who visited Cote D'Ivoire to assess English language needs and how the Council could help to meet them. We stayed in the luxurious Sofitel Hotel Ivoire, located in the chic district of Cocody in Northern Abidjan, convenient for the university, foreign embassies and the business district of Plateau. On the Sunday morning I took a walk around the lagoon and arrived at the impressive St Paul's Cathedral in time for a mass in English at 11.00 a.m. The Cathedral was completed in 1985 at a cost of US$11 million and can seat 3500 worshippers. Its dramatic modern stained glass windows include scenes depicting animal life in Africa on the arrival of the first missionaries. During the country's post-electoral violence of 2010-11, nearly 2000 people of all faiths gathered in this spot in hopes of finding safety from armed men roaming the streets of Abidjan. The struggle between rival political factions resulted in thousands of deaths, mostly civilian, and many more displaced individuals.

The Overseas Development Administration had run two very successful projects in pre-and in-service training for secondary teachers and established a network of ten ELT resource centres throughout the country. Our recommendations included a proposal for setting up a British Information Centre in collaboration with the Embassy. We could see a demand for a British Council Teaching Centre but if this did not fly we recommended providing support for the private sector. The visit ended with a reception for up to 120 key contacts in ELT, government, industry and communications organised by the Embassy, to which around 40 came. In an article for EL Gazette under the title "African Jewel Chooses English Over French,"[26] I described how demand for English was increasing dramatically. The Council had opened an office in the early 1990s but closed it nine months later at the height of an economic slump. But with a 50% devaluation of the CFA franc in 1994, exports had become competitive again and the economy was showing signs of rapid recovery. One private language school owner, Vera Miller of the English Language Institute, had opened up in January 1995 with forty students and increased numbers by 50% each term since, despite hiking fees by 30%.

In October 1995 I was invited by IATEFL Chile and the Instituto Chileno Britanico de Cultura to give a plenary talk at their 3rd IATEFL conference entitled 'Can Global Issues be Taught to Young Learners?' and a mini-course on 'Teaching Reading to Young Learners' for Cultura teachers and state university teacher trainers. The visit also included meetings on the changing role of the British Council and the development of British Studies. One of the more embarrassing moments was when I was invited for a meal at the house of the Cultura Director, Miriam Rabinovich, and inadvertently sat down on the veranda on a wicker chair which had only just been painted white and the paint hadn't yet dried. I got a white wicker pattern all over the seat of my trousers and the back of my suit jacket! On my return to Manchester I tried to claim for the cost of a new suit from the British Council, but my request was turned down.

Another challenge was presented by an invitation from Phil Mitchell, who had been the Science Officer in Brasilia and was now interim Director in Namibia, to help draw up a two-year strategic plan for English in Namibia. This was against a background of fairly savage cuts in the budget for English, and the decision by the government to change the medium of instruction from Afrikaans to English across the entire educational system. This changeover had created massive problems related to teachers' linguistic competence to teach English, and other subjects through the medium of English. There was some doubt about the future of the office and resource centre and a real risk of complete closure by 1998/99. One option I identified, perhaps prophetically, was co-location with the High Commission. This didn't happen at the time, although the British Council did move into shared premises with the Goethe-Institut a few years later, but I see that now, in 2019, it does in fact share its premises with the High Commission.

Another review was of the Council's support for ELT in Cyprus. The island had been divided by the Green Line after the Turkish invasion of North Cyprus in 1974, when the Turkish army occupied the northern third of the island. The Turkish Cypriots subsequently declared independence in 1983 as the Turkish Republic of Northern Cyprus, but were recognised only by Turkey. The British Council had an ELTO based at Eastern Mediterranean University in North Cyprus, whose name badge on his office door began with "Dr..." but this turned out to be a spurious claim, as he had never actually completed his PhD course.

One of the more extraordinary sights in North Cyprus is Varosha, the abandoned beachfront quarter of Famagusta. Prior to the Turkish occupation, it was the modern tourist area of the city. Its inhabitants fled during the invasion and it has remained a ghost town ever since. In the early 70s, Famagusta was the number-one tourist destination in Cyprus with many new high-rise buildings and hotels. Varosha in its heyday was one of the most popular tourist destinations in the world and was a favourite of celebrities such as Raquel Welch, Brigitte Bardot and Elizabeth Taylor.

My posting to Consultancy Group was supposed to be for three years. However, after only 18 months I was unexpectedly summoned one morning to a meeting with Dr Roger Bowers, the Director of Consultancy Group. After a few pleasantries he suddenly came out with, "I think you should start applying for other posts."

"What do you mean?" I queried.

"I can't tell you any more right now but your days in Consultancy Group are numbered and you need to look for another post. But please keep this to yourself as it's not yet official."

A few weeks later it was announced that the Council was abolishing Consultancy Group and cutting the number of Manchester-based ELT consultants from ten to two. I went home, told Fanta, and we prayed about what I should do next. Scouring through back issues of the Office Bulletin I found an advert for the post of Director Mozambique, for which you needed overseas experience, a background in English teaching, and a qualification in Management. As it happened, I had been taking advantage of being in the UK to do a training course and had just passed my Diploma in Management at Henley Management College. The only snag was that the closing date for applications was three weeks earlier. I phoned up the Regional Director in Harare, explained that I was very interested in the post, felt that my experience and qualifications were an excellent match, but that I hadn't applied as I was in the middle of a three-year posting to

Manchester. However, I had suddenly found myself in the position of having to apply for other jobs. He appeared quite sympathetic and explained that they hadn't yet studied all the applications but were planning to do the shortlisting the following day. "So, if you can get your application to me by close of play today, I'll consider it along with all the others. However, I must warn you that it's very competitive and we have a good range of well-qualified candidates to choose from".

I managed to get an application cobbled together that afternoon and faxed it off to Harare before leaving the office. To my surprise I made the short list, passed the interview and was offered the job to start in Maputo in three months' time.

4 MOZAMBIQUE

We then began on a flurry of preparations, shipping off our heavy baggage, looking for a suitable school for James, reading up on Mozambique and taking lessons to get the Portuguese ticking over again. We managed to secure a place for James at the American International School. This turned out to be very convenient as the rented three-storey house which we took over from my predecessor was located near the beach on the coastal road from the centre of Maputo out towards Costa del Sol, and the school was located along this road a couple of kilometres closer to the centre of town. The house was on some reclaimed land a few feet above sea level between the beach and a tidal lagoon behind the beach. This was not a problem until they tarred the road from the beach toward the lagoon a couple of blocks away, which then interfered with the drainage. So whenever there was a combination of high tides and heavy rain, the downstairs toilet, which was below the level of the rest of the ground floor, used to fill up with stinking muddy water to a depth of three or four feet.

The British Council had recently been downsized, its

general lending library closed, and the office moved from its previous location downtown in the red light district near the port to a smallish two-storied bungalow with a two-room resource centre to be focused on English teaching and management training on the upper floor, and a couple of offices, one of which had been sub-let to the Crown Agents who were bidding for a customs reform project, down in the basement. We were about to bid to manage an ODA-funded project to improve the quality of English teaching in secondary and vocational schools and my first few weeks were spend assisting with finalising the bid. Luckily we won the project, to deliver the Secondary and Technical English (STEP) Project over the next three years, in partnership with London University's Institute of Education. Without being too modest, having an ELT and Management qualified Director with African experience was an important factor in helping to secure the project. The plan was to work in partnership, with the Institute of Education delivering consultancy advice and training, VSO providing twelve volunteers to work one in each province, alongside provincial teacher supervisors, and to recruit an English Language Teaching Officer (ELTO) project manager/adviser to lead on project delivery. We were able to recruit Eddie Uprichard, who had extensive overseas teacher training experience, to fulfil this role. Eddie was quite a portly character and the Ministry of Education allocated him an office on the 21st floor of the ministry building, with a splendid view over Maputo, but he found it a bit of a struggle to climb the stairs when the lift was out of order (which was quite frequently the case). We rented a small house for Eddie and his Ghanaian wife Vida in Sommershield, and ordered basic furniture from South Africa, as there wasn't much to choose from in Maputo. The only problem was the double bed we had ordered, which Eddie insisted should be sent back and changed for king size as he and Vida were too big to fit in a standard-sized bed! The Ministry of Education appointed two counterparts to work alongside Eddie, Angela Martins, who is now Head of the Cultural Commission at the African Union in Addis Ababa, and Jose Dinis, who later left to become Director of the Instituto de Linguas in Maputo from 2000 to 2012.

According to the British Council's English Agenda website:

"The project had huge impact, influencing all areas of secondary English provision in the country.

It successfully:

- developed a team of well-qualified managers in the Ministry of Education and Provincial Directorates of Education

- revised secondary English syllabuses for Grades 7 to 11 and commissioned suitable textbooks adapted to the Mozambican context

- set up a certificated Diploma Course validated by the Institute of Education, University of London, and an Access Course for less-qualified teachers

- established English Language Resource Centres, connected to the internet, in all ten provinces of the country.

By the end of the project approximately 150 teachers had been trained to diploma level and over 300 had benefited from the Access Course. A series of secondary level textbooks was adapted by the British ELT publisher Macmillan to fit the new syllabuses, and for the first time all students at secondary level had access to the books and materials they needed to achieve success in English".[27]

Jose Dinis comments:

"The STEP Project was really very successful because we managed to set up a network of ELT resource centres in the provinces which are still being used by teachers. The model has now been replicated more widely in the system; for example the French have used the same principles and approach for a French language project in partnership with the Pedagogic University. The project provided a model for INSET and other systems of teacher support. For instance, the new Institute for Distance Education is setting up centres on the STEP model, not just for teacher training but for a whole range of distance learning courses".[28]

There was a lot of pressure on budgets in the 90s and one of the ways I devised to make some additional income was to ride on the back of the management resource centre and begin running communication skills courses for managers for a fee. These covered topics such as making presentations, telephone skills, report writing and became quite a lucrative source of income for the Council. There were some muttered rumblings of discontent from the few private language schools operating in Maputo about unfair competition, but our courses were highly targeted and offered either in-company or on our very modest premises and did not represent a serious threat.

The main opposition came from within the British Council itself. Any income-generating language teaching was supposed to come under the auspices of the Direct Teaching operation which had strict rules about how classes were to be organised (e.g. using "native speaker" teachers rather than employing locally-recruited staff). When we had a turnover of only £10-20,000 per year nobody raised an eyebrow, but once the turnover reached £100,000 p.a. questions began to be asked and I got my knuckles firmly rapped for running an illicit Teaching Centre.

However, a solution was found. The British Council had recently opened a Direct Teaching Centre in Johannesburg. Located on the top three floors of the Council building in downtown Brahmfontein, this was in an area where few people wanted to walk the streets after dark. Even the Council Director Les Phillips got mugged and robbed within a few yards of the office door. This meant that the centre, done up at vast expense, had considerable difficulty filling its classrooms and was never going to make a profit. So we were allowed to continue running our management training courses in Maputo as a satellite of the loss-making Teaching Centre in Joburg, with our profits included in their books to offset their losses.

Several years later the Council did bite the bullet and formally set up a Teaching Centre in Maputo, much to the annoyance of other private language schools. One of these, the Lynden Language School, was run by two middle-aged ladies who had spotted a lucrative market in Maputo in the early 90s. Denise Lord wrote to David Blackie several years later:

"We are a private language school operating in Maputo since 1991. About four years ago we received a visit from someone who was doing a survey on EFL teaching in Mozambique. The alarm bells should have started ringing there and then since the person involved was the wife of the then Director of the British Council in Maputo. So in our innocence (or downright stupidity) we supplied her with all the information on how we operated and subsequently were more than a little put out to find that the British Council had decided to move one up from the few scattered courses they were giving and go full on into offering courses at similar prices, timetables and even the way we split the levels,

Well to cut a long story short over the last 4 years we have written to David Green, Neil Kinnock, been to the Deputy High Commissioner and received all the wonderful reasons in the world as to why they have every right to operate as a business under the guise of a charity, not pay taxes, etc ad nauseam - this must be familiar to you.

Although we seem to have come up against a brick wall, at least where the Council are concerned, the fight does go on albeit with rest periods. Look out Council and do not underestimate the two middle-aged women running this school - we will fight the good fight and WIN."[29]

Finding competent accounts staff was a major problem in Mozambique. The British Council was still using a manual accounting system and at the end of each month the accountant had to do a trial balance. When I first arrived in Mozambique our accounts were relatively straightforward, but once the STEP project got under way they became very complex, with provincial resource centres receiving monthly advances which they had to account for in detail and problems of communication which meant that receipts and other supporting documentation often went missing in the post. There were glowing reports from a previous temporary Director on the accountant's file, saying she always managed to get the accounts to balance! I had a feeling there was something not quite right, and asked for someone to come from Johannesburg to do a detailed audit. However, as they were expecting an external audit later in the year in South Africa, it was about nine months before the Regional Accountant, Elma Wood, arrived to go through our accounts with a fine tooth comb. She discovered that the reason the accounts always balanced was because if they didn't, our accountant would just make up a journal with no supporting documentation to bring them into balance. I read the riot act to the accountant, explained that what she had been doing could be construed as fraud, and gave her a first written warning. A few weeks later she resigned. I was told that her boyfriend, an engineer who worked for BP, had threatened that if he ever came across me in the dark, he would smash me in the face!

The new accountant was keen and enthusiastic but still struggled to cope with the vagaries of the Council's arcane accounting system. Eventually I decided the solution was for the Accountant and the Office Manager, who were both in the same grade, to swap jobs. Both of them seemed happy with this, and the problems with the accounts went away. Marta Madeira subsequently went on to work for the Ford Foundation and is now a very successful HR coach and entrepreneur with her own company and an impressive list of local and international clients. In an article entitled, "Marta Tomázia Guimarães Madeira: The Mozambican with Moxie" on the "*She inspires her*" website, she gives this advice: "Find what it is that you really love to do and just start. It doesn't matter how much competition there may be - just let your uniqueness shine. "If I had known how relatively easy it would be, I would have started earlier" she says. "Provided you have clear, compelling goals, are prepared to work, lead by example, and provide value for money, you can be successful."[30]

The Accounts Assistant also proved problematic. He was frequently off sick and seemed to be getting very forgetful. On one occasion after he had been sick for several days we needed to get into the safe in his office, for which only he knew the combination. We sent a driver to collect him so he could open the safe but he couldn't remember what the combination was. So we had to get a safe cracker to come and drill a hole in it and remove the lock. It turned out he was dying of AIDS and very sadly he passed away only a few weeks later.

Mozambique became the newest member of the Commonwealth when it joined in 1995, the first member of the Commonwealth to have no historic ties with the U.K. The Guardian commented, "This was partly in recognition of the suffering Mozambique endured during the sanctions against the then Rhodesia, partly because all its neighbours belong and it seemed lonely, and partly (one suspects) because Nelson Mandela threw his influence behind the idea".[31]

In November 1999 there was a state visit to Mozambique by the Queen and Duke of Edinburgh. The shortest royal visit ever (lasting only ten hours), it coincided with a "Partnership Week" organised by the British High Commission, and we in the British Council organised a tour to Mozambique by the Caroline Taylor

Jazz Band to coincide with the trade fair, with the band playing at the opening ceremony. The stands included Armitage Shanks, displaying their latest bidet, and the University of Warwick, scouring for recruits.

We got the Duke of Edinburgh to unveil a plaque to commemorate the opening of our grandiosely-named "management training centre", two classrooms in the newly refurbished basement of the office building in Rua John Issa, previously occupied by the Crown Agents who had moved out to other premises when the refurbishment began. Some of the wiring was a bit ropey and we were slightly worried the Duke might make one of the tactless remarks for which he is famous, e.g. "Was this wiring done by Indians?" but the ceremony passed off without incident. After a couple of speeches we had a reception in the garden with several different groups of key Council contacts representing ELT, education and the arts.

The Guardian reported, "The Queen arrived in Maputo, capital of Mozambique, for a 12-hour finale to her tour of Africa to be greeted by thousands of people, all in T-shirts proclaiming their support for the ruling party, Frelimo. Buckingham Palace protested mildly, to be told that the opposition party, Renamo, had been invited but declined to attend. President Joaquim Chissano said: "This is how we welcome people in Mozambique. It's an election period, so they wore the T-shirts." The subtext was that the Queen could hardly expect the people of one of the world's poorest countries to turn up at the airport under their own steam... President Chissano said he regretted that the Queen could not stay longer because he wished to show her the sights. Maputo itself has a stunning Indian Ocean setting and a seedy post-colonial charm; the rest of the coast is said to be spectacular. The response to the Queen's visit was underwhelming. When she went to city hall to be given the freedom of Maputo a crowd of just 14 gathered in the vast expanse of Independence Place, plus about 40 baffled-looking schoolchildren who had been bussed in and handed flags."[32]

The Queen had a private meeting with Afonso Dhaklama, the leader of the opposition Renamo party. I had used our contacts in the Arts world to ensure that dancers from the National Dance Company were on hand to entertain the Queen en route to the Trade Fair, and we also got the Maputo Bus Conductors and Drivers Band to perform for her. We were asked by the High Commission to ensure that the Caroline Taylor Jazz Band who were playing in the background at the Trade Fair should make sure that they kept the volume down – "the Queen doesn't like loud music." When the Queen was introduced to Caroline Taylor, Caroline asked her, "Are you coming to our gig tomorrow night?" to which the Queen replied, "No, I'm sorry, I've got to go back and open parliament."

In the evening there was a reception given by President Chissano, to which I was invited, along with the British Council Regional Director Les Phillips who had come over from Johannesburg for the occasion. I was slightly disappointed when shortly after the visit he was given a signed portrait of the Queen, whilst I had to settle for a signed portrait of the Duke of Edinburgh. The Guardian article concluded, "Mozambique's ferocious incidence of malaria may have combined with the opening of her own parliament tomorrow to force her to rush away without even staying the night. The president said he was just glad she had come."[33]

In February and March 2000 catastrophic flooding took place in Mozambique, cutting off the main road to South Africa and making thousands homeless. The flooding was caused by heavy rainfall that lasted for five weeks and killed around 800 people. It was the worst flood in Mozambique in 50 years.

"The rainfall started on the 8th February 2000, but was not just in Mozambique. Other countries were also affected, including Swaziland and Botswana. However, it was Mozambique that was hit the worst. In the first few days, the capital city was drowning in water. But the rainfall did not cease. The rivers that ran down into the valleys were surging with water. On the 11th February, the Limpopo River overflowed, flooding villages for miles around. The Limpopo Valley suffered massive losses and damages, and disease spread through the people who were affected. Dysentery was rife. Over the space of three days, the country had experienced seventy five per cent of its year's rainfall. Still, the weather continued to batter the country. On the 22nd of the month, the coastal town of Beira was hit by an enormous cyclone. The cyclone (named Leon-Eline) caused further damage, especially from flash floods. Farms and arable land were completely submerged in the towns of Xai-Xai and Chokwe.

People were forced out of their homes, and had to climb onto roofs and into trees in the hope that they would be rescued. Over five hundred thousand people were saved this way as the waters continued to rise. The first on scene were Navy ships. However, as more and more people were affected, the South African government sent helicopters. However, despite the rescues, the government response and international aid was slow to reach the country. It was almost three weeks after the start of the flooding that rescue supplies and tools finally arrived from Western countries. The rainfall continued to hit the country for five weeks.

The damage was colossal, and the areas affected were almost completely destroyed. Farmland and crops which villages relied on for survival were submerged in the waters. Many families were totally stranded with no food or clean water, so hundreds died from starvation, and over forty health stations were completely destroyed, including the second largest in Mozambique. Irrigation systems all over the country were ruined, which was one of the main reasons for the loss to agriculture. Over one hundred thousand farming families had lost their livelihoods, with nearly fifteen hundred square kilometres of land almost destroyed. But it was not only the crops that were damaged. Twenty thousand cows were either swept away by the flood waters, or died from disease shortly afterwards. In the aftermath, four hundred and fifty million dollars was required to rebuild after all the damage".[34]

The BBC reported a dramatic birth in a tree:

"Rositha Pedro was born in a tree on Wednesday - while her mother clung for safety above Mozambique's floodwaters. Heavily-pregnant Sofia Pedro, who is in her mid-20s, had climbed to shelter in the tree on Sunday, after the rising floodwaters forced her out of her home. When a South African military helicopter arrived to rescue the dozen or so people who had taken refuge in the tree they were told she was about to give birth.

The child was born two minutes later, pilot Chris

Berlyn said. He flew back to a base camp and picked up medic Godfrey Nengovhela who cut the umbilical cord and helped as Sofia was winched to safety. "If the air force wasn't there, the baby and the mother would have been in big trouble," the pilot said. Corporal Nengovhela, who has worked as an air force medic for three years, said he had helped deliver babies before, but never in such an "unusual" place.[35]

Around the same time there was a disastrous mudslide in the Polana Canico area just below and to the east of the university, when huge gullies opened up, mud-walled houses were swept away and a large area down the hill towards the sea, including the grounds of the American International School which our children were attending at the time, was buried in mud to a depth of between 6 and 10 feet. The children were delighted when the school was closed for a couple of weeks but eventually reopened in temporary accommodation in Sommershield for several weeks whilst cleaning up operations were taking place on the campus. It was fortunate that there was a high wall at the rear of the school compound which prevented the damage from being much more serious. A football stadium nearby also disappeared under several feet of mud.

Frustrated at not being able to work in Mozambique and bored with not having very much to do (her niece Hawa was working for us as a nanny and we also had a Mozambican maid to do the housework), Fanta scouted around for something to keep herself occupied. She made a trip to China looking for things to import to either Guinea or Mozambique, and renewed her acquaintance with a Chinese entrepreneur named Zhang Bo. Together with another Guinean, she imported a container of San

Miguel beer from Hong Kong, intending to sell it to local bars at a lower cost than they had to pay for the locally-produced 2M beer. Unfortunately when I tried to offload some cases to the High Commission, it was pointed out to me that as a diplomatic passport holder, Fanta ought not to be engaging in business activity in Mozambique. So that knocked that one on the head.

Around the same time she was tempted to dabble in the trade in timber and sharks fins, which was not illegal in Mozambique. In the northernmost provinces you could buy a kilo of dried sharks fins for around US$2, and send them by airfreight to Hong Kong for US$4 a kilo, where a trader would pay $100 a kilo. I had serious doubts about the ethics of this trade, as in order to obtain the fins, the local fishermen would kill the shark, thus endangering an endangered species, but I neglected to put my foot down, something I was shortly to regret.

A recent Guardian article highlighted the issue under the headline "Chinese Appetite for Shark Fin Soup Devastating Mozambican Coastline":

"Standing among coconut and mango trees near the coast of Mozambique, Fernando Nhamussua carefully prepares shark meat for a family meal – and contemplates a basket with a profitable haul of four dried shark fins. "I want to sell them to the Chinese," the 33-year-old admits with disarming candour, estimating that a kilogram's worth will fetch around 5,000 meticals (£104). "We take them to town where there is a place for Chinese buyers. It's good money." Nhamussua reckons he has sold 20 fins so far, boosting his normal income and his hopes of completing a modest concrete house that stands unfinished. But this burgeoning trade along the

Mozambican coast is putting precious species such as manta rays in existential danger, according to local conservationists."[36]

The article goes on to explain that conservationists have called for legal protection of species such as sharks and manta rays, the banning of gillnets – which create a wall of netting to catch fish – and greater education of and alternative livelihoods for fishermen. But the fisheries ministry is powerful.

According to the Guardian, "the fishing controversy echoes wider concerns over what some in Africa regard as a Faustian pact with China. The Environmental Investigation Agency has said nearly half of the timber exported from Mozambique to China is done so illegally, costing the impoverished nation tens of millions of dollars a year."[37] Carlos Carvalho, an activist based in Maputo told the Guardian reporter, "The Chinese are gangsters and they have the protection of certain officials in Inhambane province. Every month it is escalating. Inhambane is out of control. It is the killing field of Mozambique and nobody is doing anything about it. It absolutely devastates me."[38]

I wished I had made my objections known more forcibly before Fanta made a trip to the northern provinces accompanying Zhang Bo in our Land Rover Discovery. I was at work one morning when there was a phone call from the British High Commission saying that Fanta had had a serious accident somewhere north of Inhambane – about 700 km north of Maputo – and that I needed to get there as quickly as possible. Scared of what I might find, I arranged with the High Commission to go with an embassy driver, quickly gathered a few belongings and we set off late in the morning. We had been told that Fanta had been taken to a village dispensary somewhere about 100 km north of Massinga. We drove for about 8 hours and arrived at the village after dark, around 8 p.m. The dispensary was dimly lit by the light of a single bush lamp with various patients lying on grimy mattresses on the floor. We were told that, as they had no facilities and only small supply of medications to treat common ailments, including malaria, colds, and eye infections, Fanta had been taken to a larger dispensary 50km back down the road we had just driven along. If we went about 2 km further up the road we would find the wreckage of the Land Rover. When we tracked this down, I was horrified to discover that the roof was completely flattened, down to the level of the bodywork below the windows. Fearing the worst, we drove back down the road and eventually arrived at the hospital in Massinga around 10.00 p.m. We found Fanta lying on a bed with a mattress covered in a dirty sheet and clearly in severe pain. The only painkillers they had were aspirins and she had been given the maximum possible dose. The nurse said there was nothing much they could do until the next morning when the radiographer would arrive for work and she would be able to have an x-ray. It turned out she had swerved to avoid a dog which suddenly ran in front of her, lost control, and then the Land Rover had rolled over several times before coming to a halt lying upside down on its roof at the side of the road.

The next morning we loaded Fanta onto a trolley and pushed her along an uneven path to the x-ray room. When the results arrived back, the doctor said it was not looking good. She had fractured her pelvis in four different places.

His advice was to get her to a hospital in Maputo as quickly as possible, either by an ambulance sent from Maputo, or if we could afford it, by air ambulance. The local hospital had only a makeshift ambulance in the back of an ancient Land Rover Defender and going 700km in that would be extremely uncomfortable. Fortunately we were covered by the Foreign Office medical scheme, and I managed to get through to the High Commission by phone. They were very helpful and managed to arrange for an air ambulance to fly to an airstrip around 100km away near Inhambane. It would arrive towards evening and we were to meet the paramedics at the airstrip and then fly to Nelspruit, across the border in South Africa. The pilot had been advised that the plane could fly straight to Nelspruit in South Africa without having to clear customs or immigration in Maputo, so the High Commission said they would arrange for our passports to be picked up from our house in Maputo and sent across the border to meet us when we arrived at the airport in Nelspruit.

The drive in the makeshift ambulance was excruciatingly painful for Fanta, who kept asking the driver to go slower as the road was very potholed and every bump wracked her body with pain. I whispered that he should try and get there as quickly as possible so as not to prolong the agony. After a couple of hours we arrived at the airstrip and shortly afterwards the plane landed. Fanta was pumped full of morphine and for the first time in nearly twenty four hours got some relief from the pain.

However, there was a snag. The pilot had now been told the previous advice he had been given was wrong and he would have to land in Maputo to clear customs and immigration before flying on to South Africa. We duly touched down at Maputo airport and I approached the immigration officer with some trepidation. Initially he was insistent that without passports we could not leave the country. I almost lost my cool but tried to reason with him. "If this lady dies, it will be because you are stopping us leaving." Eventually he said he was hungry. I delved into my wallet and pulled out everything I had in Mozambican meticals - around 20 dollars - and thankfully that did the trick. "O.K. you can go. Boa viagem."

Fanta was lying in the back of the plane on a stretcher being attended to by the paramedics and I was sitting in the front seat next to the pilot. At one point the single engine suddenly stopped. Terrified we were about to drop out of the sky, I asked the pilot what was going on. "It does that sometimes," he replied. "You just have to press the starter a few times to get it going again." That was the last thing we needed, a blockage in the fuel line or some other problem with the plane. Finally we reached Nelspruit without further incident, where someone handed over our passports and Fanta was loaded into the back of a waiting ambulance.

When we arrived at the Nelspruit private hospital, a further problem arose. Before Fanta could be admitted, the hospital wanted a guarantee that all expenses would be met. The High Commission in Maputo was supposed to have sent them a fax saying that Fanta was covered under the Foreign Office Medical Scheme, which would meet all her hospital expenses, but it seemed that someone in the High Commission, not realising that this was the case, had sent a fax saying the exact opposite, that all expenses were to be met by the patient/relatives. I tried to explain this was a mistake, but the admissions department would have none of it. I had three credit cards, but the £5000 deposit the hospital was asking for came to more than combined limits of all three cards. For the second time that day I found myself saying a quick prayer and pleading with the staff to admit her. I explained it could all be sorted out the following day. Eventually the hospital staff agreed to admit her, found a vacant bed and pumped her full of strong painkillers. It did seem ludicrous that, in spite of the FCO medical scheme having already spent thousands of pounds on an air ambulance to get her to the hospital, the hospital operated a pay as you enter policy and wouldn't admit her without being sure they would get their money.

The following day they took some more x-rays and confirmed that Fanta's pelvis was broken in four places and she would need metal pins inserting to hold the bones together. The consultant decided not to operate straight away, as there was a remote chance that the bones might knit back together without the need for pins. We prayed hard that she would make a full recovery. God answered our prayers and miraculously, two weeks later, she was released from the hospital without needing an operation. My brother, who is a GP, said she would most probably have very bad arthritis in her old age, but for now she was fully restored to health and strength again.

Amazingly, the car was just about still driveable, provided you went very slowly. I managed to get it back to the Land Rover garage in Maputo, but the insurance company decided it was a write-off. The following year the premium more than doubled from £800 p.a. to £1,700 p.a.

An incident which seriously damaged my reputation with the Regional Director and probably helped to ensure that I failed to get another Director's post on leaving Mozambique took place when a VIP from London was visiting South Africa. At the beginning of February we got a phone call to say that the Regional Director would be bringing the VIP over to Mozambique, arriving early in the morning and leaving late in the afternoon the same day. I arranged for various meetings and for twenty key contacts to be invited for lunch at a restaurant on Friedrich Engels Street. We booked two tables, each for twelve people. Then just the day before, there was a call from Johannesburg to say that the plans had changed and they would be arriving after lunch and staying overnight. I delegated someone in the office to phone the restaurant to change the booking from lunchtime to the evening, re-arrange the visit programme and also got them to call all the dinner guests and let them know the time had changed.

When Fanta and I arrived at the restaurant half an hour early around 7.00 p.m. it was only to discover that the restaurant disclaimed all knowledge of our booking. The first few guests arrived and hung around waiting for them to find us somewhere to sit. It was Valentine's Day, when Mozambicans all like to eat out with their husbands, wives, boyfriends and girlfriends. The restaurant was fully booked and it took forever before they eventually found some tables and chairs and arranged them on the lawn. We ordered some drinks which also took ages to arrive, and it was close to 9.00 p.m. before a waiter came and took the orders for food. Then there was another very long wait. Fanta even went into the kitchen offering to help, but was given the brush-off. Not only had the restaurant vastly over-booked, but several of their staff had failed to turn up that evening, so they were short of cooks and waiters! A few of our guests gave up and went home. We contemplated trying to find somewhere else to eat, but the local staff said that with it being Valentine's Day, everywhere else would also be fully booked. We finally got our main course around 11.00 p.m., by which time most of the guests were starving or drunk or both. All in all the evening was an unmitigated disaster!

When we first arrived in Mozambique, in late 1995, the country was quite under-developed and was still recovering from nearly twenty years of civil war, during which the ruling left-wing socialist government of Frelimo (Front for the Liberation of Mozambique) was under attack from the rebel forces of Renamo (Mozambican National Resistance). The right wing apartheid regime in South Africa as well as Ian Smith's government in Rhodesia gave support to Renamo, whilst left wing governments in Tanzania and Cuba backed Frelimo. About one million Mozambicans were killed in the fighting or died of starvation, whilst a further five million were displaced across the region. Roads and railways, schools and hospitals were destroyed and landmines scattered around throughout the country.

I visited one primary school near Inhambane where there was a very overgrown patch of scrub right behind the goal at one end of the football pitch. When I made some throw-away remark about the field looking rather neglected, the head teacher explained, "Oh, nobody can go there, it's a minefield. We keep losing footballs when they get kicked too far past the goal line."

In 1995 there were no supermarkets in Maputo, and many basic essentials were unobtainable. We used to go once a month or so at the weekend to Nelspruit, the nearest sizeable town across the border in South Africa, to stock up with supplies. At the time the road to the border was quite narrow and pot-holed and the journey to Nelspruit took some 5-6 hours. Often we would stay over on the Saturday night and on Sunday morning get up and go to church, then do the rounds of Pick and Pay filling up three or four trolleys with food and other essential supplies before having lunch and heading back to Maputo and the border before it got dark. As we had diplomatic number plates we didn't have to pay any customs duty, so it made shopping in South Africa quite cost-effective. On one occasion when we reached the border I was doing something to the car while Fanta went and joined the queue for immigration with the two children and all four passports. I arrived just as she got to the front of the queue to be confronted by a black South African immigration lady who looked at her, then the children, stared at me, then said to Fanta, "Why are you married to this white man?"

Fanta quickly retorted, "Well, this is the new South Africa – you could have one too!"

Race was still a major issue in South Africa in the mid-'90s even though apartheid had officially been done away with several years earlier. It was still very unusual to see mixed race couples and even rarer to see coffee-coloured children. In Mozambique, however, race never really seemed to be an issue. The Portuguese colonists had largely intermarried with the local people and many

Mozambicans have some Portuguese blood in their veins.

By the time we left Mozambique five years later it was visibly improving day by day. There were several new supermarkets, including Pick and Pay (the joke went "your wife picks and you pay") and a brand new two lane super-highway toll road all the way from Matola to the South African border. This cut the travelling time to Nelspruit by more than half to less than two and a half hours.

One weekend we were staying at the Promenade Hotel in Nelspruit en route to Johannesburg, as it was quite far to do the entire journey in one day. Fanta and I were in one room on the second floor with the children, and Fanta's niece Hawa, who was working for us as a nanny, was in the adjoining room. We were woken up around 5.00 a.m. to the sound of someone banging on the door. It was Hawa, yelling, "The hotel's on fire. We've got to get out quickly." There hadn't been any fire alarms, and the corridor was starting to fill up with thick black smoke. It subsequently turned out that the fire exits were locked. Marie suffered badly from asthma, so smoke was quite dangerous for her. Fanta grabbed her and headed off down the smoke-filled corridor. Meanwhile Hawa woke James up while I spent several minutes searching around the room trying to find where I had left my trousers and spectacles. We then opened the door to the corridor, only to find that it was completely full of dense black smoke. Retreating back into our room, we filled the bath up with water, soaked some towels in it and stuffed the wet towels into the gaps under and around the edges of the door. Not quite sure what to do next, we went out on to the balcony which overlooked the square down below and a small garden with an ornamental pond. Our room was over the kitchens, and I was worried there might be gas cylinders which could explode. We couldn't see round the corner of the building from where the smoke must have been coming. The square below was deserted with no sign of anyone arriving to fight the fire. After a few minutes, someone appeared down below crossing the square and shouted, "Jump, the hotel's on fire!" A piece of advice which we thought it wise to ignore. Hawa then had the bright idea of tying the bed sheets together to make a rope down which to climb, (as later immortalised in the film "Hangover 3"). We tied one end to the parapet on the balcony. We didn't have very much of value with us, only clothes, apart from a video camera I had bought the day before for the Council office. I decided I'd better not leave that behind to either burn or get stolen, so chucked the box off the balcony, along with my shoes. Unfortunately it landed in the ornamental fish pond down below and never worked again.

James set off down the rope and reached the ground without mishap, followed by Hawa who jumped off about ten feet above the ground and injured her heel. I followed them, but managed to slip several feet between one knot and the next and hurt my finger in the process. Now on the ground, I looked around for my shoes but could only find one of them and spent several minutes searching around in the flowerbeds before I managed to discover the other.

By this time the fire brigade had turned up with an extending ladder. They laid it flat on the ground and extended it to its full length, but then found it was too heavy to raise it up. I had to show them that the way to do it was to close it up again, hold it up vertically, then raise each section upwards till it reached its full height. We left the firemen scrambling up the ladder to the upper floors, then headed round the corner to look for Fanta and Marie. We could see flames shooting out through the roof of the third storey, half way along the hotel wing. Fanta and Marie had assembled with the other guests on the car park at the front of the hotel.

Eventually after the fire appeared to have been put out we were shepherded into the restaurant on the ground floor and given cups of tea or coffee. The girl at the checkout desk insisted we had to pay the full cost of the two rooms where we had spent the night. I pointed out that we hadn't spent a full night there and had abandoned the rooms half way through at 5.00 a.m., but she was adamant. I reluctantly paid up and said I would be back to speak to the manager on our return from Johannesburg! By this time it was morning and the sun had come up.

We somehow managed to retrieve our belongings and carried on with our journey to Johannesburg. Here we had booked a room on the ninth storey of a hotel. When we checked in and went up to the room I remember James saying, "I hope we don't have to escape from this hotel down knotted bed sheets."

A couple of days later my ring finger began to swell up very badly. It was so badly swollen that I couldn't remove my wedding ring. I went to the hospital where they cut off the wedding ring, did an x-ray and said I had broken the bone in my finger. It needed two metal pins inserting, which they were able to do the following day, but despite having physiotherapy for several weeks back in Maputo, until today I still can't bend the finger fully. Some time later we returned to the Promenade Hotel, where the wing where the fire had broken out was completely closed off for repairs and repainting. I asked to see the manager, who refunded the cost of our rooms for the night and agreed that they would pay for the wedding ring to be welded back together, although they flatly refused to pay for a new one. For some time after this I avoided staying on upper floors when I checked into a hotel.

It transpired that the fire had broken out in a room on the ground floor occupied by an Indian family, although the exact cause of the fire was never revealed. Probably they were either cooking in their room or had hung their washing to dry on the electric fire, which had then overheated.

At the weekends we often went to the beach at Macaneta, about an hour's drive north of Maputo and accessible only with a 4 x 4 vehicle after a ferry crossing near Marracuene. It was pretty much undiscovered though there was a bar and some beach huts at Jay's, run by a middle-aged couple who had bought up a stretch of sand dunes next to the beach several years earlier. Sometimes we stayed overnight, and one memorable morning we were woken up quite early by the owner asking if we could help to jump-start his truck because the battery had gone flat. Trying to tow a truck then jump-start it in six inches of soft sand is virtually impossible. After pulling it up and down the stretch of sandy road near the camp for a couple of hours we were just about to give up when suddenly the engine started.

James had a quad bike which he used to race around Bairro Triunfo where we lived and along the beach near

Costa do Sol, which occasionally we took with us to Jays. He did pretty well driving it through the sand as a 9 or 10-year old.

Another favourite place to spend the weekend was Mlawula Nature Reserve just across the border in Swaziland. Here there was a small round hut for cooking with four tents perched on the edge of a steep drop down to a river several hundred feet below. There were plenty of wildebeest, impala, kudu, snakes and tortoises roaming around and if you were really lucky you might see a leopard. Usually we had the place entirely to ourselves. One of the most impressive facilities was the shower, perched on the edge of a precipice with a pole to hold the shower rose up in the air, and a metal sleeve surrounding the central pole. You lit a fire using wood and kerosene at the bottom of the pole and after a few minutes hot water came out of the shower at the top.

We were fortunate in having the Kruger Park just over the border to South Africa, en route to Nelspruit. One of Africa's largest game reserves, it has the big five - lions, leopards, rhinos, elephants and buffaloes and literally hundreds of other mammals, birds and reptiles. The park includes very diverse habitats including mountains, forests and plains, and you can either stick to tarred roads or drive off into the bush. It also has a very wide range of places to stay from luxury safari lodges to primitive tented camps.

To celebrate the millennium in December 2000 we went on a massive overland trip from Maputo to Cape Town, staying in various places en route, including Port Elizabeth, Knysna with its oyster farms, and Durban. On the night of 31st December 2000 we stayed on the 22nd floor of a hotel overlooking Durban's South Beach and got a splendid view of the fireworks going off all around the bay. A couple of rockets even landed on our balcony! Highlights of the trip included following the Garden Route, and in Cape Town visiting Robben Island and climbing Table Mountain. We had a scary moment or two when we stopped at the side of the road in the middle of the Karoo desert and found the car would not start. We were miles from the nearest village and there was very little passing traffic. We decided I had probably flooded the engine, so waited a few minutes and tried again. Still it refused to start. After half an hour or so, Fanta said, "Let me try." Immediately the engine sprang into life. When we reached Cape Town we took it to the Land Rover agents but they couldn't find anything wrong. It still had an intermittent fault, so when we eventually got back to Maputo we changed the starter motor, which seemed to resolve the problem.

One of the strangest places we visited was Beira, Mozambique's fourth largest city and a port which serves the landlocked countries of Zambia, Zimbabwe and Malawi. At one time it was the favourite holiday destination for white Rhodesians. A stark reminder of that time was the Grand Hotel, built in 1954 and operated until 1974, when it was closed due to lack of guests. The building was used as a military base during the civil war and is now said to be home to over 3500 squatters.[36] After Frelimo assumed power in 1975, the bar at the swimming pool became the office of Frelimo's Revolutionary Committee, which was responsible for establishing socialism in the province of Sofala. While the main hall of the Grand Hotel was used for party meetings and events, the basement became a prison for opponents of the new government.

After 1981, Beira became a haven for refugees from the civil war seeking safety and access to international aid. The Grand Hotel became a refugee camp with most of the refugees coming from rural areas. The story goes that some refugees who arrived during the night were overwhelmed in the morning by the view of the ocean, which they had never seen. They tried to walk towards the sea but, never having been in a multi-storey building and not understanding the height differences, they fell to their deaths from the roof terrace. Now occupied by squatters, the once elegant rooms are full of rubbish, with leaking rain water, open elevator shafts and inaccessible stairs. The heavily polluted Olympic swimming pool is used for bathing by inhabitants who cannot afford to buy water at the privately owned water pump opposite. There is said to be a high risk of cholera, diarrhoea, HIV/AIDS, malaria and scabies amongst the squatters. The water supply, sewer pipes and electrical wiring have all been removed and sold in order to obtain money for food and water, while the parquet floor was used as fuel for cooking.

North of Beira the shoreline has an extensive collection of shipwrecks, many dating back to colonial times, including one right under the shadow of the Macuti lighthouse. There is also an impressive area known as the ship graveyard. Vessels that were sabotaged by the Rhodesians in 1977 or sank due to being unseaworthy have been towed here and abandoned.

Another interesting spot which we once visited for a run with the Hash House harriers is Xefina Island. At low tide this is only around 2 or 3km from Costa do Sol. It was used as a leper colony in the 19th century, then early in the 20th Century the Portuguese built an army base and fort to protecting the approach to the city of Maputo. In the years leading up to independence, it was used by the Portuguese as a concentration camp for political prisoners, with stories of dungeons below ground level being used exclusively for torture. On the far side of the island are the ruins of enormous gun batteries built by the Portuguese to defend Maputo Bay during the first and second world wars. These massive cannons and lookout towers are now completely in ruins and crumbling into the sea.

In Sierra Leone I had owned a windsurfer. When we first arrived in Maputo I contemplated getting one to surf in the sea off Costa do Sol. However, when I saw the size of a shark caught by the fishermen at Costa do Sol - it was about one and a half times the length of their boat - I rapidly had second thoughts.

Often in the evening after work I would take Speedy, our Dachshund, for a walk along the beach to Costa do Sol, stopping for a beer on the balcony of the restaurant or at the little shack opposite, which had an area fenced off with a few chairs and tables on the edge of the beach. Other places began to spring up in the dunes between the beach and the main road, which in places was starting to get seriously eroded. Once when we were at the beach with James and Marie, Speedy wandered off, and next thing we knew someone had grabbed him and was running off down the beach towards Maputo with him under their arm. I gave chase, eventually managed to catch up, and grabbed Speedy back from the thief, who claimed he thought the dog was lost!

Pets generally caused us some heartache in Maputo. There was a goose which we had bought intending to have it for dinner but didn't have the heart to eat, after Marie became quite attached to it. So for several weeks it became a pet. However, it made such a mess of the area around the swimming pool that it did finally end up in the cooking pot. We told Marie we were having chicken for lunch that day.

On taking over the house we inherited thirteen tortoises from my predecessor, most of them giant tortoises like you find only in a zoo. Unfortunately Speedy developed a habit of stalking them, waiting till they poked their heads out from under their shell, then biting the head off. By the time we left there were only six survivors. Six were despatched by Speedy, and the seventh was found one morning lying upside down in the swimming pool. It must have fallen in, then been unable to climb out again and sadly had drowned.

There were also two cats, not very domesticated, who used to turn up to be fed then spend the rest of the time roaming around the nearby gardens. Unfortunately one fell foul of the Rottweiler which lived next door and got practically torn limb from limb. We managed to rescue her and took her to the vet. He didn't hold out much hope but he managed to sew her up and to our amazement she made a remarkable recovery. But after that she gave next door's garden a very wide berth.

There was a little nameless restaurant a couple of miles beyond Costa do Sol which had a mural on the wall depicting the plane crash in which Samora Machel died in mysterious circumstances in 1986, where we sometimes went at weekends for a fried fish lunch. There was also a fish market along the Marginal near the American School where you could get the most delicious prawns and crab cooked to order. You bought what you wanted to eat in the market, then took it to one of the little stalls at the back of the market for it to be cooked.

Bilene, about two hour's drive north of Maputo, has a beautiful beach although it is quite far off the main road. One weekend we rented a small apartment there, and in the morning headed off down to the beach. There is a freshwater lagoon which stretches several miles out into the Indian Ocean. We were sitting up the beach on the dry sand and James and Marie were paddling around near the water's edge, when they suddenly shouted out for us to come and look at something. Lying on the edge of the water face down was a girl aged about fourteen or fifteen, who appeared to be completely drunk and not moving. I didn't like to turn her over in case she suddenly woke up and accused me of molesting her, so I just poked her gently with my foot, but there was no response. Realisation gradually dawned that she was unconscious and most probably dead. We summoned help and took the children off to another part of the beach for the rest of the morning. It turned out that there were three sisters who couldn't swim, and who had walked very far out into the lagoon, where the water is quite shallow for a couple of kilometres, then suddenly shelves very deeply. They had got into difficulties and couldn't get back into their depth, and sadly all three drowned. This put a bit of a damper on the rest of the weekend by the sea.

We had been in Maputo for five very happy years and it was time to apply for other jobs. The Regional Director told me at the annual performance review not to expect another Country Director post – clearly he was intending to spike my guns.

Not knowing where we would be in a year's time we decided we should take advantage of the fact that the Council paid boarding school fees and enrol James in a prep school back in Britain. In September 2000 we sent him off with some trepidation to Kingsmead School in Hoylake, near where my brother Ian and his wife Julie lived. He survived the first term without mishap, and at Christmas came out to Maputo for our marathon road trip to Cape Town. Not long after we left Maputo he developed acute diarrhoea, and when we reached Cape Town we took him to hospital and they did various tests. Unfortunately we had to leave Cape Town on our way back to Maputo before getting any of the results. His tummy seemed to settle down, so we packed him off to boarding school for the start of the second term.

About three weeks later we got a phone call in the middle of the night from my brother saying he had been rushed into hospital and operated on for appendicitis, but when they removed the appendix it didn't seem to solve the problem. For a couple of weeks he was on a drip and not eating anything. Fanta flew back to be with him and a week later when he still wasn't eating the British Council agree I could fly back also. As soon as I arrived he perked up and began to eat again! There was some doubt about what was wrong with him, and we thought it could be at least partly due to being away from his family, so we took him out of the boarding school and he spent the final two terms before we left Mozambique back in the American School. By this time, however a diagnosis of "ulcerative colitis" had been confirmed. He was given prophylactic medicine to take twice a day and the likelihood was that he would have to take medication for the rest of his life. Fortunately this turned out not to be the case and a few years later he had fully recovered and was gradually weaned off the medicine

Meanwhile I was looking for another post within the Council. I applied for what looked like a fascinating newly-created post as manager of the "Peacekeeping English Project". This would mean moving to London, which Fanta seemed to be quite happy about as it would be much more cosmopolitan than Exmouth where I had owned a flat before we got married, or Chester, where we now owned a house. I had some reservations - with two small children, (Marie was now 7 and James 11) - it might be quite difficult for Fanta to work, and my salary would just about cover the rent in London and not very much more.

5 LONDON

We got the packers in once again and despatched our sea freight, arriving back in the U.K. in September 2001. After prolonged discussion, the British Council's Human Resources department accepted my argument that because when I worked in Manchester, unlike most of the staff who had moved up from London, I had not qualified for "detached duty", (because we had already owned a house within commuting distance of Manchester), now that I was being posted to London I should be entitled to be treated the same way as the other staff and given detached duty in London. It turned out there were a small number of precedents for this and so, although they tried their best to wriggle out of it, they couldn't really refuse to pay towards our rent.

The rulebook also said that if you were posted back to London, they would continue to pay the boarding school fees for up to three years, provided you were expected to eventually move overseas again. We tried to get them to agree to let James return to his prep school, but they argued that as he was not in the boarding school on the date we left Mozambique, they were no longer obliged to pay for school fees. Knowing what I know now, with hindsight, I should have got the PCS Union to take up his case, but as we were already doing battle with the Council over paying towards the rent, we caved in.

We booked a cheap hotel in South Kensington for a couple of weeks through the Council's hotel booking department and spend several days doing the rounds of estate agents. At first we started looking in Putney and other places quite close to central London, but gradually realisation dawned that you couldn't get anywhere reasonable in a respectable area for less than around £2000 a month within ten miles of central London. So we lowered our sights and started looking further out. We finally found a three-bedroomed town house in Ham, half-way between Richmond and Kingston, for a slightly more affordable rent, and the Council agreed to pay a rent allowance of £1000 per month towards this. It was in Ashburnham Road, where one end of the road was Council housing and flats, and the other end a private development. We were not to know that the Council housing end was pretty rough - for several months the local bus drivers refused to drive down the road because vandals kept throwing rocks at the buses!

After several days in the South Kensington hotel, both the children developed a measles-like rash all over their bodies. It was only when we looked under the beds (they had been playing on the floor) we discovered that the entire area was absolutely swarming with fleas. We complained to the manager and they moved us to another room, but it was several weeks before the children stopped scratching and fully recovered. The Manager did agree that, in view of the unfortunate circumstances, they would waive the charge for the room for the entirety of our stay. When I visited South Kensington a few years later I noticed that the hotel had closed down and the building was boarded up awaiting demolition.

The next challenge was to find schools for both the children. There was a primary school at the end of the road, but it was over-subscribed. We eventually got a place for Marie in a lovely little primary school in Petersham, a picturesque village between Ham and Richmond. Greycourt Secondary School at the end of our road had places in Year Seven and a good Ofsted report from several years earlier, so we enrolled James there. Six months later there was another Ofsted inspection and the school was put into "special measures".

Finding a local evangelical church was another challenge. There was a small church in the next road but they didn't have any young people. We eventually settled for Canbury Park Church in Kingston, where we were given a warm welcome. James, who by now was quite an accomplished drummer, used to play the drums for the Sunday morning service.

The Peacekeeping English Project, financed by the Foreign Office and the Ministry of Defence through the "Conflict Prevention Fund", was operating in twenty-two countries stretching from Estonia in the west to Turkmenistan in the east. Its main aim was to enable peacekeeping forces - mainly military but increasingly civilian forces such as police and border guards - to communicate more effectively through English and thus contribute towards conflict prevention, or where conflict already existed, as in the former Yugoslavia and Central Asia, to its eradication. Nearly all the countries involved in the project were members or aspiring members of NATO and the EU, or members of Partnership for Peace, a NATO-inspired initiative to bring together different armies for joint peacekeeping exercises. For this they needed English, which (together with French) is the lingua franca of NATO. In Eastern Europe and the former Soviet Union, Russian had been the lingua franca of the military, but with the collapse of communism and Soviet hegemony in the region, a resurgence of ethnic nationalism, and the revival of local national and regional languages, English had become the language of choice for 'interoperability' - jargon for doing joint peacekeeping exercises, anti-terrorist and anti-trafficking activities and relief operations.[40]

The project had become very successful in a short period of time, largely because it was so necessary. The people who were learning English needed it urgently. They were highly motivated and using it in real, sometimes even life or death, situations. Silvija Simane, who ran the Baltic Battalion Language Centre in Latvia, where students from all three Baltic States were working together to improve their English, told me, "We are not just teaching English. We are changing mind-sets, taking responsibility for our own learning, developing cultural awareness and building effective teams."[41]

During a visit to Uzbekistan towards the end of 2001, Deputy Minister of Defence Kayumov commented, "After eighty years of Soviet domination, we are keen to learn as much as we can about democratic Western approaches and methods. It is absolutely vital for the survival of Uzbekistan that senior officers are exposed to Western ideas and influences. Only in this way can Uzbekistan fend off the threat of extreme Islamic fundamentalism."[42]

These words perhaps sound a bit hollow in the light of the revelations subsequently made about Uzbekistan's human rights record by Craig Murray, one of the youngest people to become a British Ambassador (at the age of 43), the following year. Murray repeatedly complained to the Foreign Office that intelligence received by the CIA from the Uzbek government was unreliable because it had been obtained through torture. In October 2002 he gave a speech at a human rights conference in Tashkent, hosted by Freedom House, which broke with all the established principles of Foreign Office diplomacy. In his speech, Murray said:

"Uzbekistan is not a functioning democracy, nor does it appear to be moving in the direction of democracy. The major political parties are banned; Parliament is not subject to democratic election and checks and balances on the authority of the electorate are lacking. There is worse: we believe there to be between 7,000 and 10,000 people in detention who we would consider as political and/or religious prisoners. In many cases they have been falsely convicted of crimes with which there appears to be no credible evidence they had any connection. [43]

According to The Times, he went on to say:

"The terrible case of (two men) apparently tortured to death by boiling in water is not an isolated incident. Brutality is inherent in (your) system."[44]

It was not just the Uzbek officials who were stunned; [the US ambassador] Herbst and his fellow US diplomats were said to be "livid". Uzbekistan - which shares a border with Afghanistan - had only recently agreed to a vast US air base being built on its soil. Just a year before Murray's speech, it provided the Americans with a vital northern base from which to launch attacks on Osama Bin Laden and the Taliban. The Americans were understandably anxious not to cause offence, but Murray's graphic charge sheet made Herbst look like a fool. "The Americans prefer to carry out diplomacy like this behind closed doors," said one human rights worker. "They were aghast... For some time Murray's communiqués to the Foreign Office had been generously laced with his frank views on Uzbekistan's human rights record. Many bounced straight back to him because the London e-mail system would not accept any memo containing the word "bollocks". However, his candid reports had generally been welcomed. Clare Short, the former secretary for international development, said: "His telegrams were strong and clear because the level of repression and corruption in Uzbekistan is dreadful. I thought: this is a good guy."[45]

It was probably because the Americans were so upset that London snapped and launched an investigation into Murray's conduct in the summer of 2003. He was falsely accused of 18 separate charges including drunkenness, womanising and "unpatriotic" behaviour. Amongst other things, he was accused of seducing visa applicants in his office and going out in the embassy car "with the flag up" to tour Tashkent's late-night drinking dens. He was even alleged to have driven an embassy Land Rover down a flight of steps. None of these charges were eventually proven but he was still accused of having brought the Foreign Office into disrepute and removed from office. There is no doubt he made enemies. The Guardian reported that Chris Hirst, the embassy's third secretary, was accused by the local authorities of attacking local Uzbekistanis on the streets of Tashkent often accompanied by his baseball bat and rottweiler. The authorities had been pushed into making formal complaints against Hirst. While he was out of town, a complaint got through to Murray and he had him immediately sent back to London. Subsequently Hirst resigned.[46] The Guardian also reported that his driver was said to have driven an embassy Land Rover down some terraced steps to get to a lake shore on an Embassy picnic. "He was just showing how well-built the British car was," joked one friend. "I heard another senior embassy official drove another one down there immediately behind him. But he wasn't disciplined." Yet Mr Murray was called back from holiday to London, and threatened with demotion or the sack.[47]

There is no doubt he enjoyed touring the red light areas of Tashkent. In his Who's Who entry, he listed his recreations as "drinking and gossiping." It was on one of these nights out that he met an English teacher, Nadira Alieva, in her early twenties, who was working as a belly dancer in a night club. He separated from his first wife Fiona Kennedy and when he left Uzbekistan in October 2004, Alieva joined him in London. After his divorce was finalised in 2008, Murray married Alieva in May 2009; they have a son.[48]

Murray was removed from his post in October 2004 and sacked in February the following year. As an ambassador he could be surprisingly outspoken, controversial and undiplomatic. His wardrobe included a flamboyant collection of Wallace and Gromit and Dennis the Menace ties. He told a Guardian reporter, "People come to me very often after being tortured. Normally this includes homosexual and heterosexual rape of close relatives in front of the victim; rape with objects such as broken bottles; asphyxiation; pulling out of fingernails; smashing of limbs with blunt objects; and use of boiling liquids including complete immersion of the body. This is not uncommon. Thousands of people a year suffer from this torture at the hands of the authorities."[49] A later report by European investigators found that Uzbekistan was used as a base in the American programme of extraordinary rendition during the war in Afghanistan and Iraq, which remained secret during Murray's time in the country, because such countries were tolerant of the use of torture. He gave this as a reason to Kevin Sullivan of *The Washington Post* in June 2008 to explain why the response to his revelations was so "ferocious".[50]

I met Murray at an Embassy cocktail party he was hosting in 2003, not long after the incidents involving the Rottweiler and the Land Rover being driven down the steps. He seemed more outspoken than the normal run of ambassadors, and it was clear that there were pro- and anti-Murray factions in the Embassy and more widely in the British community. The British Council Director at the time, Neville McBain, appeared in private to side with his detractors. In late 2004 Murray Keeler moved on from his post as PEP manager and was replaced by Alan Rutt. A couple of years later the PEP project was suddenly closed down unilaterally by the Uzbek government with no prior warning.

My first overseas visit in my new role as project director was to Latvia, where something of crisis was looming which tested my diplomatic skills to the limit.

The UK-recruited PEP manager had seriously injured his leg when he fell down the stairs at his block of flats on the way back from the celebrations at the Queen's Birthday Party. After he had been on sick leave for four months, the Defence Attache had written to the Ministry of Defence, criticising the British Council for failing to provide a substitute, condemning the manager as ineffective and demanding that he be replaced. The Defence Attache also made some totally unwarranted accusations about sexual orientation as grounds for dismissal, which I had to point out went against the Council's diversity policy. By now the manager was back at work, though still on crutches, and together we devised a six-month action plan with some very specific objectives, outputs and deadlines. I got the Defence Attache to agree to the plan, on the understanding that if things didn't improve we would take further action down the line. Fortunately everything came together, the manager succeeded in achieving all the objectives we had agreed within the time-frame, succeeded in gaining the confidence of the DA and even managed to secure additional funding which doubled the Latvia project budget. Two years later, he organised a project wide managers' conference in Latvia which was voted "the best PEP conference yet".

My heart sank when the British Council Events Management Unit recommended a venue in East Croydon for the very first PEP managers' conference I was involved in, during the summer of 2002. For most people,

Croydon conjures up a vision of 1930s semi-detached urban sprawl and badly designed government buildings staffed by grey and faceless civil servants. Croydon is the archetypical outer London concrete jungle. As I wrote in the PEP Newsletter,

"It was a very pleasant surprise to discover that the Selsdon Park Hotel was an imposing Jacobean mansion - a superbly equipped conference centre, set in a beautiful park with rolling hills and woodlands. It has an 18-hole golf course and a leisure centre with sauna, steam bath and an indoor pool. The hotel even has its own resident ghost, known as the 'Grey Lady.' She is said to appear intermittently, dressed in Tudor or Elizabethan clothes, and occasionally surprises unsuspecting guests by walking right through their beds and melting through the bedroom wall. According to the manager, she appears to be cut off at the shins, with her feet below floor level. He thinks that this is because the level of the floor was raised when central heating was installed some years ago. Sounds plausible.

We arrived to find a large inflatable cliff had been erected in the car park. This turned out to be part of a teambuilding event for BBC Worldwide, whose staff were expected to scale the wall in an effort to become happier and more efficient workers. It looked like hard work. Our programme began to look pretty tame in comparison."[51]

The conference aimed at encouraging networking and exchange of best practice. It was also a chance for the clients, FCO and MOD, to explain their policies and strategy, in a session led by Lt Col Steve Balm of the MOD's Central and Eastern European Directorate. It was also the first such conference where country-based staff had been represented. Roma Valiukiene (Lithuania), Ilona Rozyska (Poland) and Katerina Zagortcheva (Bulgaria) helped to redress the age and gender balance slightly and brought a fresh perspective to the discussions. We also had presentations from providers of longer courses in the UK and USA: the Defence School of Languages represented the UK military English establishment and Elaine Hutchinson from the Defence Language Institute at Lackland Airbase in Texas gave a presentation about the programmes offered there. David Riley from Macmillan outlined their plans to produce a series of Military English textbooks, tentatively called "Campaign", and Andrew Stokes from Clarity in Hong Kong spoke about their computer-authoring packages.

One matter which was not included in the conference report was the amazing capacity which the participants demonstrated to knock back the alcohol. I had agreed that we would provide the equivalent of half a bottle of wine each for the opening dinner. However, about half-way through the first course, the Head Waiter came up and informed me that the wine had run out. I told him to just carry on serving and to add it to the bill. A couple of weeks later I got a call from the British Council's accounts department who had received an invoice from the hotel which included 95 bottles of wine at around £18 per bottle. They were querying whether this was correct as the dinner was for only 50 people. I had to agree that it was, and made a mental note to ration consumption more strictly in future.

The following year we held the annual conference in Moscow. This seemed a logical venue given that we had projects all over eastern Europe and the former Soviet

Union. On arriving at Sheremyetovo airport all the other passengers on the plane sailed through immigration with no problems. When I arrived at the front of the queue, the immigration officer input my passport details then said, "Would you mind stepping to one side for a few minutes?" and disappeared off with my passport. After what seemed like a couple of hours wait - but was probably only 45 minutes - she reappeared, handed me my passport and said, "OK, you can go now." I could only assume that the FSB was keeping an eye on us - or was I just being paranoid? People I knew who worked for the Teaching Centre in Moscow have told me about returning home to their flats and finding muddy footsteps in the hallway, or items moved around from their normal place. It was assumed the FSB had let themselves in and snooped around, and deliberately left some evidence of their visit just to let the teachers know they were being watched and not to step out of line.

At this time the MOD had high hopes of starting a PEP project in Russia, with a manager/trainer posted to the St Petersburg Naval Academy, but alas this was not to be. After an incident in 2006 involving a rock in a Moscow park used as a dead drop, relations went decidedly cold. The BBC reported, "A former UK government official has admitted Britain was caught spying when Russia exposed its use of a fake rock in Moscow to hide electronic equipment. Russia made the allegations in January 2006, but this is the first time anyone in the UK has publicly accepted them. Jonathan Powell, then Prime Minister Tony Blair's chief of staff, told a BBC documentary it was "embarrassing", but "they had us bang to rights." He added: "Clearly they had known about it for some time."

Russian TV showed a video of a man walking along the pavement of a Moscow street, slowing his pace, glancing at a rock and slowing down, then picking up his pace. Next the camera films another man, who walks by and picks up the rock.

The Russian security service, the FSB, linked the rock with allegations that British security services were making covert payments to pro-democracy and human rights groups."[52]

One of the more fascinating projects was in Turkmenistan. The PEP manager, Mark Calderbank, became romantically involved with a Turkmen national of Russian descent, named Tatiana, whom he eventually married. Turkmenistan at the time was ruled by Saparmurat Niyazov, otherwise known as Turkmenbashi, or the father of all Turkmen. One of his edicts, intended to prevent local women from being exploited, was to demand that any foreigner wishing to marry a Turkmen had to make a (non-returnable) deposit of US$50,000 as well as to have owned a house in Turkmenistan for at least a year. Mark's successor as PEP Manager in Ashgabat writes, "I didn't know about the $50,000, but I did know that he came from a banking family and inherited something quite significant when he was in his sixties. I believe that he divided his time between Turkmenistan and France after retiring".

"For anyone interested in matters developmental, Turkmenistan offers a very interesting example of outcomes. Of the several people I worked with and I believe as a direct result of project activity, my immediate boss was initially promoted to major, then demoted to captain before being killed in a highly suspicious traffic accident. My closest counterpart, who obtained a Chevening scholarship to study in the U.K. whilst with the project, successfully completed an MBA degree before setting up in partnership here in the UK in a carpet retail business, which expanded to two big shops before he sold his share and returned to set up what is now Ashgabat's main foreign language school. I did some distance teacher development for his school last year. I was invited back, all expenses paid, but refused as I couldn't stand the thought of all the vodka! One of our centre's instructors became Minister for Defence after the project was closed down and another took over as director of the languages centre in the Military Academy, which I believe continues to operate in brand new Academy premises, before being appointed as Defence Attache to Belarus. It was also the case that only during the latter part of the PEP phase were both we and the Embassy's Defence Section able to get Turkmen military participants to attend foreign events. Once the project ended, so did all approvals for military to travel outside of the country unless sent by the ministry itself. Several of our former students are now senior officers, although what they think of their exposure to western education and ideas I don't know, but I think it is fairly true to say that few if any of those outcomes could have been predicted from the project design document!"[53]

I visited Ashgabat a couple of times during my four years as PEP Director, and it never ceased to amaze me. True to Leninist-Stalinist tradition, there were statues of Turkmenbashi all over the capital, Ashgabat. One of the weirdest was a thirty-foot tall statue of a rampant bull, with what appeared to be a solid stone globe about 50 feet in diameter balanced on the bull's horns, slightly fractured at the top representing a disastrous earthquake which had devastated Ashgabat in 1948. On top of the globe was a stone statue of his mother, and in her arms an effigy of a little golden child (Turkmenbashi himself).

Another enormous gold plated statue of Turkmenbashi sat astride three sloping pillars and revolved so that his face was always facing the sun. Known as 'the Tripod', it was built in 1998 to commemorate the country's official position of neutrality. The 75m structure was topped by a 12m gold-plated revolving statue of Niyazov. In 2010 it was dismantled and moved by Turkmenbashi's successor to a new location in the southern part of the city.

Turkmenistan has the world's fourth-largest natural gas reserves, more than the United States, but it isn't exactly spreading the wealth. Much of the population outside the capital is impoverished. Ashgabat is blisteringly dry and hot for most of the year, dumped in the middle of the desert. It also holds the record for the highest density of buildings made from white marble in the world.

According to Wikipedia,[54] Turkmenbashi was "one of the world's most totalitarian, despotic and repressive dictators. He imposed his personal eccentricities upon the country, such as renaming Turkmen months and days of the week after members of his family and local fruits. In 2005, he closed down all rural libraries and hospitals outside of the capital city Ashgabat, in a country where at that time more than half the population lived in rural areas, stating that, 'If people are ill, they can come to

Ashgabat.' Under his rule, Turkmenistan had the lowest life expectancy in Central Asia".

Amongst his more eccentric decrees were laws banning the use of lip syncing at public concerts in 2005 as well as sound recordings on TV, at all state sponsored cultural events, and public weddings and celebrations. He banished dogs from the capital Ashgabat because of their "unappealing odour." Right-hand-drive imported cars which had been converted to left-hand-drive were banned due to a perceived increased risk of accidents. After Niyazov stopped smoking in 1997 following heart surgery, he banned smoking in all public places and ordered all government employees to follow suit. Chewing tobacco on Turkmen soil was later banned as well. He outlawed opera, ballet and circuses in 2001 for being "decidedly unturkmen-like" and in February 2004 decreed that men should no longer wear long hair or beards. Gold teeth were discouraged in Turkmenistan after Niyazov suggested that the populace chew on bones to strengthen their teeth and lessen the rate at which they fall out. He said:

"I watched young dogs when I was young. They were given bones to gnaw to strengthen their teeth. Those of you whose teeth have fallen out did not chew on bones. This is my advice." He abolished the Turkmen word for bread, replacing it with *Gurbansoltan*, his mother's name, which also became the word for the month of April.[55]

According to an obituary in The Independent, "Niyazov, who once openly compared himself to a deity, even stipulated what exactly it meant to be "old". Childhood lasted until 13, he decreed, adolescence until 25 and youth until 37. Old age, he insisted, did not begin until 85. Following in the footsteps of China's Mao Tse-tung, Niyazov published his own version of the Little Red Book. Called the Rukhnama, the 500-page tome of spiritual musings was said to be "a moral guide" for Turkmens and was required reading on school and university curricula. A mixture of revisionist history, his own poetry and spiritual musings, the book and its teachings effectively became a new religion replacing the ideology of Lenin, Marx and Engels. It was also a way of ensuring that the mostly Muslim nation did not embrace Islam as strongly as other nations in the region: Niyazov was a fierce opponent of Islamist radicalism, seeing it as a threat to his own hegemony.[56] New governmental employees were tested on the book at job interviews and an exam on its teachings was a part of the driving test in Turkmenistan.

In 2003, due to an oversight, the Foreign Office omitted to budget for its £1.3 million share of the overall £3 million annual project budget. When this came to light in mid-year, the Foreign Office wrote to the ambassadors in 10 Eastern European countries including Poland and the Czech Republic asking what the effect would be of terminating these projects at short notice. It was a considerable challenge to get the funding restored. I collated impact statements from the project managers in each affected country and prepared briefs on the negative impact of early termination, including a brief for the British Council Director-General, David Green, who was meeting with the Permanent Under-Secretary at the Foreign Office and the Chair of the Commons Foreign Affairs Committee. Jeff Hoon in his role as Secretary of State for Defence took the matter up with the FCO at ministerial level. The eventual outcome was very positive for the project - not only was the FCO's funding restored, but for the first time it was guaranteed for three years, rather than being reviewed annually. It also led to the project expanding and extending the successful model developed in Europe and Central Asia into a global project by 2006/7.

In May 2009, however, the Guardian reported that the future of PEP projects was in doubt. Most of the original projects were planned as three year interventions after which they would be handed over to the host nations. According to Max de Lotbiniere, "Next month, four of the current nine PEP programmes will shut with just a few weeks' notice as a result of cuts in Britain's conflict prevention budget, raising concerns about the future of remaining programmes and the ability of partner countries to maintain specialist language training. The PEP programmes that are due to close are in Bosnia and Herzegovina, Vietnam, Guatemala and Colombia. In March ministers announced that due to the increased demand on an annual budget of $839m allocated to conflict resolution (not including the British military presence in Iraq and Afghanistan) and the fall in the value of the pound, money would be diverted to frontline UN and EU peace keeping missions, such as Darfur and Somalia, and away from other support programmes. The government has provided an additional $107m to offset these cuts but this is not enough to save peacekeeping training in Central America and elsewhere".[57] This was particularly unfortunate for Colombia, where the programme had only just started and was seen as a vital tool in the war on drugs.

It seemed to me that the golden age for Peacekeeping English managed by the British Council had been when the funding was controlled by the Ministry of Defence and the Foreign Office. After the MOD put its funding into the Global Conflict Prevention Pool, it lost some degree of control over how the funds were spent, allowing DfID, with its focus on development aid and with an overt anti-military bias, to influence the agenda. The writing for PEP projects around the world in the longer term was now on the wall.

Sometimes projects I helped to design took a long time to come to fruition. An example was the project with the police in China. I had carried out a scoping visit to China in 2004, visiting Beijing, Xian and Shanghai, accompanied by the Defence Attache, but it would be four years before a project at the China Peacekeeping Police Training Centre would get off the ground.

I don't think I have ever eaten so much in my life as I did that week in China! It seemed to be a constant round of banquets, often 12 or more courses, and accompanied by vast amounts of alcohol. To begin the dinner, the host (at the "head" of the round table) toasts 2-3 times (depending on how formal the dinner is). Further toasts happen throughout the meal - it does not just occur at one particular time. So, people are constantly getting up to toast each other. If you are a guest, someone might ensure that your glass is always full. It is entirely possible to end up drinking too much, if you are not paying attention. A highlight of the trip was visiting the site in Xian where the famous terracotta warrior army was discovered in the 1970s.

Whilst I was managing this project I had to do a great deal of travelling - much of it to countries which required a visa - so I acquired a second passport. Whilst I was using one, the other could be sent off for a visa for the next country I would be going to. The British Council gave a frequent traveller allowance to staff who were away from home for more than 150 nights per year, which meant I had to keep a careful record of when I was away. One year it totalled 180 days out of the 210 working days in the year.

Fanta would sometimes complain that I would set off on a Sunday afternoon to visit a project then return on Friday night or Saturday with a suitcase full of dirty washing, before setting off again the following week. At one point, after our dream house by the sea in Guinea got commandeered by one of the President's four wives, she was away in Guinea for an extended period trying to get the house back, leaving me to juggle with the demands of looking after two children as well as giving my full attention to the job!

There was an interesting legal battle involving James, which eventually reached the High Court. One of the subjects he had opted for at Grey Court school was Russian, and he was on the way back from a school trip with his teacher and classmates to the School of Oriental and African Studies in central London one day in April 2005. On their return, quite late in the afternoon, the teacher told them they could make their own way home from Richmond station. James decided to go with his friend to buy a CD he wanted. They looked around the record shop for a few minutes, but when he opened his wallet he realised he didn't have enough to pay for it, so put it back on the shelf. They then went for a walk along the bank of the Thames, and noticed they were being followed by someone in a black uniform, who eventually accosted them and told them he was a Community Support Officer and that they were behaving in a suspicious manner. After demanding their names and addresses, he then gave them both a piece of paper which said they were banned from returning to the area for the next twenty-four hours. Failure to comply with this order could lead to a £2000 fine or three months in prison.

James arrived back home quite distressed, and I fired off a letter to the editor of Private Eye, and at the same time wrote to Liberty, the Human Rights organisation, setting out what had happened and arguing this was a gross infringement of individual liberties. Private Eye published the letter, but nothing was heard from Liberty for several weeks. Then there was a phone call from one of their lawyers, Alex Gask, saying that they were very concerned about the government's policy on Anti Social Behaviour Orders (ASBOs) and were looking for a test case to take to court. Would James agree that they could take up the matter on his behalf? James seemed to be quite happy for them to do so and he gave them a lengthy statement outlining what had occurred. I sought an assurance that there would be no costs involved for us personally. Liberty said they would apply on James' behalf for legal aid. This was normally refused but they would appeal and it was normally granted on appeal.

In May 2005, the Guardian reported, "Police powers to return teenagers to their homes under "draconian" antisocial behaviour laws were challenged yesterday in a landmark case that could curb child curfews across the country. A 15-year-old boy from Richmond-upon-Thames, south-west London, told the high court that the creation of two "dispersal areas" in his neighbourhood infringed his human rights, preventing him from going to band practice, walking the dog and running errands for his mother. The court heard that more than 400 dispersal areas have been set up in England and Wales under the 2003 Antisocial Behaviour Act, giving police officers sweeping powers to disperse troublemakers and forcibly take under-16s home. Encompassing parks, bus stops, cinemas, railway stations and other public places, the zones are designed to prevent antisocial behaviour and intimidating gatherings of young people. As well as dispersing groups of more than two people within the designated area, the zones give police and community support officers the power between 9pm and 6am to forcibly remove anyone they believe is under-16 and unaccompanied by a responsible adult and return them home.

The teenager whose complaint led Liberty, the human rights group, to bring its application for a judicial review of the curfew and dispersal orders, lives in a dispersal zone in Richmond. The boy, known only as W and described as a "model student", said his social life had been curtailed by the creation of the dispersal area and he was afraid he would be "pounced on" by police and returned to his home. He used to take a bus once a week back from band practice at a local church but became dependent on his parents for a lift so he did not break the curfew.

"I resent having to be taken home because I feel I am old enough to be independent," he said in a written statement read out in court. "I'm worried about being [picked up and] taken home by the police when I've done nothing wrong. I'm also worried that if I am taken home by the police other people will see me and think I have done something wrong." He described how he would no longer meet friends out on the street, walk his dog, or visit the local Tesco to buy milk for his mother after 9pm because he was afraid of being stopped and marched home by police.

Javan Herberg, for W, told Lord Justice Brooke, sitting with Mr Justice Mitting, that while such restrictions could appear trivial they were a fundamental part of becoming adult and prevented families from making responsible decisions about their children's rights and freedoms. "These are important parts of growing up. Small journeys to the shops are important stages in developing independence from the family." Alex Gask, Liberty's legal officer, said: "There is a real danger of sweeping 'anti-yob powers' demonising an entire generation of mostly decent kids."

Liberty is arguing that the curfews infringe four articles of the Human Rights Act: the right to liberty, respect for private life, the freedom of assembly and freedom from discrimination."[58]

The case dragged on for several weeks, pending the judge arriving at his decision. Then in July 2005, the Guardian reported under the heading "Teenager Wins Legal Fight Against Curfew":

"A teenager was today given the legal right to challenge one of the key planks of the government's antisocial behaviour agenda. The high court judge decided, in what is being seen as a landmark ruling, that the 15-year-old boy - known only as "W" - can challenge the legality of child curfew zones created by the government in a bid to crack down on antisocial behaviour.

Two high court judges granted "W" a declaration that the police have no power to use force to remove young people to their homes under the legislation. Lord Justice Brooke and Mr Justice Mitting, sitting at the high court in London, said: "If parliament considered that such a power was needed, it should have said so, and identified the circumstances in which it intended the power to be exercised."

The Richmond teenager, who has the backing of the human rights group Liberty, and who was described in court as a "model student", had argued that the "anti-yob" legislation should not be used to penalise innocent young people. He went to the high court in May, challenging the decision by the Metropolitan Police to create two child "dispersal areas" where he lives in the London borough of Richmond upon Thames. The boy had argued that the curfew regime violated his rights to liberty under four articles of the European convention on human rights. But the Home Office disagreed, arguing that he had no standing to bring a claim as he had not been stopped by police and deprived of his liberty inside a dispersal area. In a statement after the ruling, the teenager said: "Of course I have no problem with being stopped by the police if I've done something wrong. But they shouldn't be allowed to treat me like a criminal just because I'm under 16."

The Home Office said that it would be appealing against the decision. It said in a statement that the ruling did not affect those curfew zones already created under the legislation or prevent further zones being created in the future. Police would still be able to disperse groups, it said. But the Home Office said the ruling did affect the police ability to use the law to take children home.

The statement said: "We believe the police should have reasonable force to take children home otherwise the police cannot do anything if children refuse to be taken home." Alex Gask, the Liberty legal officer who is acting for "W", said: "This is a victory for the presumption of innocence and the right of everyone, no matter what their age, not to be subjected to coercive powers without good cause."[59]

Perhaps coincidentally, for several weeks whilst this case was on-going, a police car was stationed in the road just opposite our house. This seemed to be the kind of minor harassment or surveillance you would expect from the FSB if you were living in Putin's Russia, but not what you would normally expect in a quiet suburban street in Ham. Before the case reached the High Court, they had also slapped a dispersal order on our road - Ashburnham Road - but nowhere else nearby, in addition to the zone along the river bank in Richmond.

The Daily Telegraph, which took a decidedly pro-ASBO stance, reported, "The Home Office will appeal against a High Court ruling yesterday that effectively demolished a key plank of its anti-social behaviour strategy. Judges ruled that police have no power to enforce the removal of under 16s who are out late at night in designated town centre curfew zones if they are behaving lawfully.....W's father was angry and complained to Liberty, which brought the case under human rights legislation, though the court said common law already allowed people to move around unmolested by the police if they were behaving lawfully...Tony Arbour, the leader of Richmond borough council, said he was "very disappointed" by the judgment. 'This was a useful tool in our armoury to keep Richmond the safest borough in London. This has more or less neutered the power we had. Youngsters may well stick two fingers up at police who ask them to disperse.'[60]

The Court of Appeal eventually upheld the High Court's decision. Liberty reported on its website, "The following year the Court of Appeal dealt a severe blow to curfew powers when it ruled that the police only have the power to use force to remove children who are involved in, or at risk from, actual or imminently anticipated bad behaviour."[61]

One of the delights of living in Ham was that Richmond Park was just down the road and the river Thames was a stone's throw away. We tried to make the most of our time in London, with so many things to do and see at weekends. I soon realised that it was quicker to cycle the fifteen miles to work than to go on the bus to Richmond then the tube to Charing Cross. By bus and train it could take anywhere from an hour and ten minutes to an hour and a half, but by bike it was always an hour and fifteen minutes give or take a few minutes depending on which way the wind was blowing. The cycle route took you through Richmond Park, along the river bank to Putney, across Putney Bridge, along some back streets to Chelsea, then you could ride (illegally but many cyclists did so) along the Embankment pavement as far as Waterloo Bridge. In the winter Richmond Park was closed to traffic after dark, and it was eerily quiet and almost magical cycling along in total darkness for several miles with only an occasional deer sitting in the middle of the path and the odd cyclist coming in the other direction. Only once did I get knocked off, by a lorry turning left right in front of me, but fortunately suffered no ill-effects. I often used to take the dog for walks along the river bank, and on one memorable occasion was cycling along the bank with the children in mid-winter when there was a lot of ice and snow about, when for some reason one of the children decided to walk out onto a frozen pond, but the ice cracked and they both fell in. The pond turned out to be quite deep and I jumped in to rescue them, getting soaked to the skin in icy cold water. We raced home as fast as we could and fortunately none of us caught pneumonia. In the summer we used to go fishing in the river and it was surprising how relatively unpolluted it appeared to be.

6 NEPAL

For the previous four years as the Peacekeeping English Project Director, I had had a great deal of responsibility and autonomy. During this time I had staved off the threat of closure in 10 Eastern European countries and more or less single-handedly scoped new projects in twelve others, so that by the time I moved on there were projects in 34 countries, and PEP had gone global. I managed the project's finances to the tune of £3 million per year and kept the clients (FCO and MOD) happy with the Council's overall management of the project. I had also set up a new coordination system for training, testing to NATO standards and materials development. So it was a bit of a let-down to find out I would be moving to a new role, based in Kathmandu, Nepal, as the "Regional Change Programme Manager".

This was to be the first time I had had a post in the Council which was entirely internally focussed, with little or no interaction with the Council's external clients and customers. The Council was about to launch out on a portfolio of several far-reaching internal change projects and my task was to work with the project teams in the

Central and South Asia region to implement these successfully. The Council had bought into a fairly tram-lined programme management system devised by the Office of Government Commerce, set up in 2000 under the Treasury to make government more efficient. The organisation acted as sponsor for best practice of project, programme, risk and service management, including a methodology called "Managing Successful Programmes" (MSP). The Council recruited thirteen of us to act as programme managers within the overall programme, including one in each of the seven regions into which the Council had divided up the world at that time, and sent us off to be trained in MSP methodology. In 2011 the OGC was closed down and its areas of responsibility farmed out to Axelos, a joint venture company, between Government and Capita Plc, to manage, develop and grow the global best practice portfolio. Before that, the OGC achieved notoriety when it unveiled a new logo in 2008. The Telegraph reported, under the headline 'OGC unveils new logo to red faces',

"It cost £14,000 to create, but clearly no-one at the smart London design outfit that came up with the new logo for HM Treasury thought to turn it on its side.

The logo as it was intended:

The logo, for the Office of Government Commerce, was intended to signify a bold commitment to the body's aim of 'improving value for money by driving up standards and capability in procurement'.

The logo rotated through 90 degrees
Instead, it has generated howls of mirth and what is likely to be a barrage of teasing emails from mandarins in other departments. According to insiders, the graphic was already proudly etched on mouse mats and pens before it was unveiled for employees, who spotted the clanger within seconds."[62]

A few weeks before we were due to leave London for Kathmandu, the British Council sent me on a five-day course run by Parity on Managing Successful Projects. The course was pretty intensive but the hotel had a spa and sauna and I spent several minutes at the end of each day relaxing in the sauna. A few days after arriving home my leg began to swell up and became extremely stiff and painful. I phoned my GP brother, who said I should go to the nearest Accident and Emergency department forthwith. The doctor at the hospital in Kingston immediately diagnosed cellulitis, gave me a course of antibiotics, and told me to keep my leg elevated for several days. This was problematic given we were in the throes of packing up ready to leave for Nepal, but the leg was so painful I really had no option. According to my GP brother, in the days prior to the discovery of antibiotics cellulitis was normally fatal.

The Central and South Asia Region was a somewhat illogical fusion of seven Central and South Asian countries – Uzbekistan, Kazakhstan and Afghanistan in Central Asia, and Nepal, Iran, Pakistan and Bangladesh in South Asia. There were few direct connections between the countries in Central and in South Asia. So when we organised a meeting of regional staff, for example, this usually had to take place in Qatar or Dubai, outside the region. The Council had decided to co-locate the Regional Office and newly appointed Regional Director, Dr. Morna Nance, in Kathmandu within the existing Nepal British Council. So to some extent as "regional" staff, we were squatters within the Kathmandu office, with me as Morna's bag carrier.

The portfolio of projects included Human Resources - mainly reducing the number of low-grade staff in Pakistan and Bangladesh and using the savings made to create a small number of posts in higher grades; Customer Service Excellence, to improve customer facing services in the region; Product Development, where a small number of large scale global and regional projects would replace a proliferation of low-cost low-impact country-based projects; the introduction of a new financial system; online regional collaboration sites including a regional intranet, and an overall Strategic Review of the region. Some of the projects, especially those involving restructuring and redundancies, were quite controversial. But Kathmandu was a pleasant enough place to live, with a vibrant culture and fantastic scenery.

On our arrival we moved into the house previously occupied by the Country Director, which still had a few months to run on the lease. This was in a spectacular location half-way up the Shivapuri mountain range beyond Budhanilkantha, several thousand feet up a mountainside overlooking Kathmandu, which was about 10 miles away. The main attraction in the temple at Budhanilkantha is an impressive 5 metre long reclining statue of Vishnu that floats in a sacred tank in the middle of the village.

The only snag was that we had enrolled the children in the British School, which was on the opposite side of Kathmandu. So the children had to get up very early in the morning to go to school, and the journey often took over an hour each way. With the lease about to expire, Fanta spent several weeks scouring Kathmandu looking for somewhere better which was also closer to the British School. After having looked at 30-40 different houses, she eventually found one which was ideal. Located near the zoo in Jawalakhel, a ten to fifteen minute walk from the school, about the same time on a bicycle to the British Council office, it was a well-built fairly modern three-storey house with five bedrooms, three bathrooms and a large garden. The only problem was that the landlord wanted $1000 dollars per month more than the British Council was prepared to pay. We put in our offer of $1800 per month and reconciled ourselves to having to carry on house-hunting. But to our great surprise, a week later we heard that the landlord had happily accepted our offer and we were able to sign a lease for the next couple of years. James had the top floor all to himself, with a bedroom, study and bathroom, while our bedroom was opposite Marie's on the first floor, where we also had a couple of guest bedrooms.

One feature of the house was a thermometer-like needle on the staircase wall, which was the earthquake alarm. This was supposed to give you at least 30 seconds warning of an impending earthquake. However, it was so sensitive that there were frequent false alarms when heavy lorries went past in the main road, about 100 metres away. We also had a tin trunk, kept in the garage, which contained 5-litre bottles of water, a radio, torches and batteries, tins of beans and corned beef, and other iron rations. The idea was that in the event of a severe earthquake such as the one which later hit Kathmandu in 2015, we would have basic supplies to keep us alive for a couple of weeks until help arrived.

We were fortunate - there were only a few minor tremors during our two years in Kathmandu, but nothing really serious. The worst incident was in September 2011, when a Nepalese motorcyclist was driving past the British embassy with his eight-year-old daughter on board. Part of the high wall around the Embassy compound collapsed in earthquake tremors, killing them both. The BBC reported that "Lawmakers in parliament hurried out of the building shouting when the quake struck in the middle of a debate on the budget."[63]

But the earthquakes that struck on April 26 and May 12, 2015 caused around 9,000 deaths, and around half a million families in the central region of the country lost their homes. As well as houses, dozens of Kathmandu's heritage buildings were destroyed, including the iconic Dharahara tower. In the quakes' immediate aftermath, relief and rescue work began swiftly, with local volunteers working with the army and international aid workers.

In order to get to Pakistan from Nepal, you had to fly via Delhi. The first time I visited Islamabad, the return flight to Delhi was cancelled at short notice and Pakistan Airlines said they would re-route me via Karachi and put me up in a hotel at their expense for the night. The overnight accommodation at Karachi airport hotel was decidedly fourth-rate, but I was sure I would survive the night. On the off-chance I decided to phone up Marcus Gilbert, the British Council Director in Karachi whom I knew from Manchester, to see if he was free to go out for a meal or drink. When he heard I was staying at the airport hotel he said, "Don't move. Don't even set foot outside your room. I'll send a driver to get you. You're not allowed to stay the night in the airport hotel – it's far too dangerous. You can come and stay the night with us!"

The British Council had closed its public access library in the wake of the September 11 attacks and moved to new premises within the grounds of the High Commission with high levels of security. According to the 2014 Global Terrorism Index, "Terrorism in Pakistan has a diverse array of actors. In 2013 there were 71 suicide attacks responsible for around 2,740 casualties. Of all attacks 16 per cent occurred in the second largest city of Karachi."[64] Karachi was said at this time to have the third highest level of terrorist "chatter" in the world, after Iraq and Afghanistan.

We spent a very pleasant evening drinking in the British Embassy club. I got the impression that living in Karachi could be quite difficult at times. Marcus's wife was not allowed to leave the Embassy compound, even just to walk a couple of hundred metres down the road to see a friend who lived nearby, without being driven in a vehicle and accompanied by an armed guard - such was the perceived level of threat. She had been caught a couple of times setting off to the friend's house on foot, and Marcus had been warned that if it happened again they risked being sent home.

My old friends from Brunei, Ralph and Lan Stather, came out for a holiday visit accompanied by their artist friend Chris Hollis. We spent the first few days exploring the sights of Kathmandu with them and cycling to some of the nearby villages. Then a few days after their arrival, a dawn to dusk curfew was imposed within the ring road around Kathmandu, with protestors burning tyres and generally creating mayhem. We had booked to stay for a few nights in Dhulikhel so we had to get up very early in the morning to beat the curfew, and found that we were virtually the only guests in the hotel, with magnificent views over the Himalayas all to ourselves. On the way to Godawari we came across a road blocked by burning tyres and had to turn back and find an alternative route.

So we basically spent the time driving around the Kathmandu valley outside the ring road while Kathmandu burned. Paul Routledge describes how, "On 22 April 2006, hundreds of thousands of people filled Kathmandu's 27 km long ring road, effectively encircling the city. Amid road blockades, burning tyres, liberated spaces and destroyed police posts, the demand of the protestors was for a democratic republic, in a country that had experienced persistent political corruption, a ten-year Maoist insurgency and a royal-military coup. For 19 days in April 2006, Nepal witnessed a popular uprising against the royal-military coup staged by King Gyanendra in February 2005. The Jana Andolan II (People's Movement II, named after the first people's movement of 1990) demanded a return to democracy, the establishment of a lasting peace in Nepal and more political and economic inclusion for the various ethnic and caste groups historically marginalised in Nepali society. The movement was successful in toppling the King's direct rule of the country, forging the way for the reinstatement of political parties, the establishment of an interim government and a more democratic form of government in Nepal."[65]

A crisis had developed when, in June 2001, the entire royal family were massacred and the king's brother, Gyanendra, assumed the throne. A state of emergency was declared, the King dissolved parliament and in October 2002 dismissed the Prime Minister and the elected government and assumed executive authority. This then stoked the flames of Maoist insurgency. In February 2005 the King assumed total control in what was effectively a royal-military coup. Following this there was a clamp-down on civil and political society: leaders of political parties and human rights organisations were arrested; journalists arrested and the offices of publications critical of the take-over raided. The main political parties put aside their political differences and formed the Seven Party Alliance (SPA), a coalition of seven political parties seeking the re-introduction of democracy. Meanwhile, the Maoists responded to the royal coup during February and March 2006 by organising a succession of general strikes, shutdowns and blockades at the local and regional levels. For19 days in April 2006, "road-blocks were organised by protestors, police posts were set aflame and martyrs of the movement (i.e. those killed by security forces) were commemorated at road intersections with flowers, the burning of incense and the displaying of photographs of the deceased".[66] In May, the newly constructed House of Representatives (i.e. the parliament) unanimously voted to strip the King of many of his powers, depriving him of any role in the state, and brought the army under civilian control. Then in June 2006, an eight-point agreement between the SPA and the Maoists committed all parties to a competitive, multiparty democracy; the upholding of civil liberties; the rule of law; and a request to the United Nations to assist in the management of arms and armies in the peace process. An interim constitution was framed in order to form an interim government.[67]

Some days during the curfew the weather was unbearably hot. A couple of hundred metres away from our house, across the nearest main road, there was a hotel called Shaligram which had a swimming pool. I am told that one day I headed off down the road with my trunks and towel, declaring, "I don't care if there's a shoot to kill curfew, I'm going for a swim at Shaligram!"

One of our favourite places to spend the weekend was the former British Ambassador's retreat, perched on a hilltop with spectacular views over the snow-capped Himalayas. Embassy and British Council staff could book to stay there at no charge. Around 1850, the Rajah had given the British Resident an indefinite and free right to use a spectacular site in the nearby village of Kakani, about 30 kilometres north-west of Kathmandu. Here a Resident not long afterwards built a spartan bungalow as a retreat from the city. This was seriously damaged in the 2015 earthquake. [68]

Another amazing place to visit was the Chitwan national park, where we took a canoe trip along the river which was swarming with mugger crocodiles. The park is host to more than 700 species of wildlife including the Bengal tiger.

On Saturday afternoons I usually went for a run with the Himalayan Hash House Harriers. This usually attracted a motley crew of around forty to fifty runners, roughly half Nepalis and half expatriates, including the US ambassador and two 14- or 15-year old Nepali boys who were known as the "hash scholars", who had joined in the run one Saturday afternoon when it passed through their village and after that kept on coming each week, usually travelling to the hash by bus. Most of the Nepalis were extremely fit, and the runs could be very long, sometimes lasting for up to three hours. The very first time I went, I tried to keep up with the runners, but it was an impossible task! So after that I went with the walkers. Even walking could be pretty strenuous, as practically nowhere in the Kathmandu valley was flat and often the trail went up and down steep mountain paths. Regular hashers were given politically incorrect nicknames such as Keeled Over, Rotter or Doggy Style. These names were either dealt out arbitrarily or after something bizarre that happened on a run. According to the hash website, "Except when Keeled Over or Yogi Hare are laying the paper, the Saturday Mixed Hash involves a run of from one to two hours duration mainly off-road, with blazing sun, sometimes with deep river crossings and, in the monsoon season, deep in mud. Hills of both the up and down type do not impede the Himalayan Hash House Harriers. But wait, don't be put off. While the hashers who call themselves runners will do the whole course trying to look like they aren't walking, real walkers are mostly able to keep up due to the Hare's clever laying of paper and judicious choice of short-cuts. After everybody gets back to the start, which usually happens, refreshments are taken, followed by certain quaint but enjoyable rituals which cannot be described here."[69] Fanta acquired the hash name "Leechscreecher" after one particularly memorable hash where she kept getting attacked by bloodsucking leeches. Usually I would take our cocker spaniels, Luke and Josh. One Saturday Luke disappeared half way round the run. It transpired he had been dognapped by a villager who had taken a liking to him. Fortunately one of the hashers had seen him being dragged off into a hut, and we were able to track him down and recover him.

On a trip to Pokhara, the second largest city in Nepal and main tourist destination, we took our driver and one of our two maids along with us. The maid started behaving very oddly and one morning accused the driver of having tried to molest her during the night, which he vociferously denied. Then after breakfast she could not be found anywhere but eventually turned up having grabbed some cleaning materials and a toilet brush and decided for some unknown reason to go and clean the bathrooms in the hotel. In the car she kept saying all kinds of strange things, so when we reached Pokhara we put her on a bus back to Kathmandu with instructions to go and see the doctor. It seemed she had had some kind of nervous breakdown and we had to dispense with her services while she underwent treatment at our expense.

The biggest success of my time in Nepal was contributing to making the case in the regional Strategic Plan for a substantial increase in the regional budget from 2008-9. This document was very well received in London and meant that the regional government grant for the British Council increased from £8 million to £11 million p.a. at a time when in most regions it was being cut, and in Western Europe reduced to zero. A National Audit Office report in 2008 recorded that the regional budget allocated for Central and South Asia had increased from £2.7 million in 2000-1 to £10.5 million in 2008-9.[70] It was time to move on.

7 BOTSWANA

Several months before my three-year posting to Kathmandu was due to end I starting looking around for other posts, especially those which could utilise my extensive experience in English language teaching. I applied for and landed the post of Regional English Manager for Sub-Saharan Africa, based in Johannesburg. However, it soon became obvious that the transfer to South Africa was not going to be at all straightforward. Under South African immigration law, if you were not going to be diplomatic, your employer had to prove that "despite a diligent search, the prospective employer has been unable to find a suitable citizen or permanent resident with qualifications or skills and experience equivalent to those of the applicant."[71] I submitted all the required paperwork, but after a few months was told that in view of the difficulty they were having in obtaining a working visa, the decision had been taken to re-locate my post to Gaborone, the capital of Botswana. This turned out to be a blessing in disguise, as Gaborone was a short half-hour flight from Johannesburg but was a much more pleasant place to live, with a low crime rate and much greater quality of life than would have been the case in Johannesburg.

We looked into the options for secondary schooling in Botswana. James was just about to start his "A" level course, and Marie was about to move from primary to secondary level. There was a secondary school with a good reputation at Maruapula, but after much heart-searching we decided the best option was to send them both off to a boarding school back in the U.K. The British Council would cover the cost of the boarding school fees, which for the two of them would come to significantly more than my annual salary, and they would get a generous allowance covering travel to Botswana in the school holidays. And if, after Botswana, I was posted back to the UK, the Council would be obliged to carry on paying Marie's school fees for up to three years provided I was intending to move abroad again within the next five years. We were anxious to find a boarding school with a Christian ethos, and narrowed the choice down to five schools. During a trip to the UK in April 2007 I visited the two schools closest to London, where they both still had friends from the time when we had lived in Ham, and we came down in favour of The Leys School in Cambridge. This was a Methodist foundation with both a strong Christian ethos and a track record of good academic results. My brother and his wife were very kind in looking after them during half term holidays when it would not have been cost-effective to travel all the way to Botswana for just a few days.

Marie took to boarding school like a duck to water. In fact seven years later in the upper sixth she ended up as Head Girl. It was much more problematic for James, who had enjoyed extensive freedom living at home and attending the British School in Kathmandu, to put up with the petty restrictions of boarding school life. For most of the first term when his friends were allowed out to explore Cambridge for a few hours on a Saturday afternoon, he spent the time in detention after being found playing computer games under the bed sheets after lights out, or other minor infractions of the school rules. In April 2007 I wrote to the Headmaster at The Leys, Mr Slater:

"We were very concerned to hear that James had been caught smoking on the roof on the last night of term. My wife and I have talked to him at length about the need to obey the school rules, hand in his work on time, take a more serious attitude to his studies and not allow himself to be led astray by his peers. I hope that this will have been a wake-up call and that there will be no further problems with his attitude and behaviour."

In Gaborone we found an unfurnished house with a swimming pool to rent in Tutume Road, two minutes' walk away from the perimeter fence of the Gaborone Game Reserve. We begged and borrowed various items of furniture from the Council Director, and were given an allowance to buy various essential items such as a cooker, freezer, sofa and beds.

'Chapel-goers appear to run in families, like asthma' wrote George Eliot in an ironic comment in *The Mill on the Floss*. Having made a conscious decision at the age of around seven to put my trust in the Lord Jesus as my Saviour and accepted that He is "the way, the truth and the life," in my boyhood and teenage years, I belonged to an assembly of the Christian Brethren in Hoylake, something which I look back on with gratitude and some degree of nostalgia. During the course of my Council career, I had been an Anglican, then a Lutheran in Tanzania, Fanta and I had been Baptists in Sierra Leone and The Philippines, and we had attended International English-speaking churches in Brazil, Mozambique and Nepal. During our four years in London, we reverted to my Brethren roots and attended Canbury Park church, a Brethren assembly which had an enthusiastic but ageing and declining membership despite all attempts to expand, including hosting a Korean fellowship on Sunday afternoons. However, this church has now successfully turned a corner and reversed its decline by amalgamating with the non-denominational Cornerstone church in Kingston and now seems to be thriving.

So when we first arrived in Botswana and discovered there was a Brethren assembly just round the corner from our house, we decided to check it out. In 1984 Dr Clark Logan and his wife Hazel had moved to Gaborone and held meetings in their home, in prisons and other parts of Gaborone. A church building was erected in Broadhurst in 1987 and had attracted a sizeable congregation. The Logans were very welcoming and invited us for lunch, but there were a couple of snags. One was that the church services were in Setswana, of which we only had a very rudimentary grasp. The other was that although we explained that we were believing Christians, we were asked to sit at the back of the church and "observe" during the "breaking of bread" (communion) service, rather than taking part in it.

We eventually settled on the lively English-speaking Open Baptist church a couple of miles away in Maruapula, led by Pastor Norman Shaefer, who is now the senior pastor at Kimberley Baptist Church in South Africa, and Desmond Henry, now a pastor at Ridgecrest Church in South Africa. Here we found a spiritual home for the duration of our stay in Botswana.

The British Council in Botswana was located in a former garage on the ground floor of the British High Commission building in the centre of Gaborone. I soon settled into my role as the Regional English Manager for Southern Africa. A major task was taking the leading role in developing a English Language Teaching strategy and implementation plan for Southern Africa (which at the time meant South Africa, Angola, Namibia, Botswana, Zambia, Zimbabwe and Mauritius). It was a challenging task to prepare the ground for the roll-out in Southern Africa of the twelve Global English products for teachers and learners which were replacing local projects in each country. One of my colleagues, Adam Dalton, wrote, "Paul has been the most proactive of the Regional English Managers in the network... Already, Southern Africa is ahead of other regions in terms of rollout and representation to ministries and other stakeholders and partners."

The High Commission building in Botswana had three floors, the top floor of which was largely unused. In the closing days of apartheid in South Africa the High Commission had had many more staff, as Botswana was a convenient location from which to keep a close eye on South Africa just across the border. When the number of Council staff grew, and there was a shortage of office space, it was decided that I should move up to an empty office on the deserted floor of the High Commission. So I existed in splendid isolation with the sick bay next door and five or six empty offices along the corridor!

One of the challenges I had to cope with was being put in overall charge of the Teaching Centres in Mozambique and Mauritius. Despite the earlier opposition I had encountered to running revenue-earning ELT programmes when we were in Maputo, the Council now had a flourishing Teaching Centre there, which had outgrown the tiny premises in Rua John Issa and was renting classrooms offsite. It was a steep learning curve getting to grips with the details of Teaching Centre Financial Plans and Client Service Standards!

There were plenty of opportunities to travel. I spent a week in Angola investigating opportunities for the British Council to set up a Teaching Centre in partnership with a local supplier, and looking into the English training needs of the training wing of the Angolan National Oil Corporation. This led to a proposal for a certificated CELTA training course for their teachers. During my first year, other visits took place to the Teaching Centres in Mauritius and Mozambique, to South Africa, as well as to the Democratic Republic of Congo, where there was a Peacekeeping English Project managed by Angus Dalrymple Smith, an ELT qualified locally-recruited manager who reportedly felt quite isolated, having had little or no contact with his previous line manager. My earlier experience with PEP centrally in London came into its own here.

On the first visit I made to DRC I had been assured that it was dangerous to go anywhere on your own and that the Embassy would send a driver to meet me at the airport, which was about an hour and a half's drive from the centre of Kinshasa on a good day. The flight from

Johannesburg landed around lunchtime in the middle of a torrential tropical rainstorm. I made my way through customs and immigration, expecting to see an Embassy driver waiting with a sign with my name on it in the arrivals hall. No such luck! I hung around for half an hour or so, then, the rain having gone off, ventured outside into the car parking area. Here I was besieged by a mob of taxi-drivers, all anxious to grab my bags and drive me into town. Thinking the Embassy driver might have been delayed in traffic or had a puncture, I fended them off and told them that someone was coming to pick me up. An hour or so passed, with no sign of a driver. I borrowed a mobile phone and tried calling the Embassy, but as it was a Saturday all I got was a recorded message saying that the Embassy was closed and would be open again at 0800 a.m. on Monday morning.

As I had been assured that someone would meet me, I hadn't asked the name and address of the hotel which the Embassy had booked me into. So eventually I collared one of the less thuggish-looking drivers and asked how much he would charge to take me to the centre of Kinshasa. Eighty dollars. I suspected I was being ripped off, but there wasn't much alternative. I told the driver, "OK, but I'll ask them when we arrive what it normally costs." So we agreed he would take me to the largest hotel in central Kinshasa which was closest to the British Embassy. Off we went. On the way I remembered the story my brother had told me about his journey to the airport when he was leaving Kinshasa after three months at a remote mission hospital in Katanga province, doing his elective as part of his training to be a doctor. They kept getting stopped at roadblocks and he was starting to worry about missing his flight. At one particular roadblock the soldiers were going through everything with a fine toothcomb. When he complained he was going to miss his flight and told them his destination, the soldiers said, "Oh, don't worry, that flight crashed on landing!"

We had been driving for at least an hour and a half. I was starting to get worried that perhaps I was being hijacked, when we pulled up outside the Grand Hotel. The driver came with me to the reception and said something to the receptionist in Lingala, and the receptionist promptly assured me that $80 was perfectly ok for a foreigner. It had been quite a long drive and I wasn't going to argue!

I gave the receptionist my passport and kept my fingers crossed that this was indeed the right hotel. She went into a bit of a kerfuffle for several minutes with two or three other staff, then eventually came back and presented me with the key to a room on the tenth floor with a splendid view over the Congo River about half a mile away in the distance.

The next day, Sunday, I decided to take a walk down to the river bank which I could see from the hotel balcony. I had got quite close to the river when I was stopped by some guards at a roadblock who wanted to see my papers. I explained in broken French that I was a visitor and was looking for the way to the river. One of them got quite aggressive, but the other told me I was on the road to the presidential palace and no visitors were allowed. So I beat a hasty retreat and eventually found another road which took me to an area with several embassies, but no obvious access to the river!

On the Monday morning I contacted the Embassy.

They said they had been expecting me on Sunday, not Saturday, and had sent a driver to the airport on the Sunday morning but he had failed to find me. I then realised that this explained the consternation when I had arrived at the hotel, as my booking had been for the next day. They arranged to pick me up and took me to the Embassy, where I met Angus and got briefed on the programme he had arranged. This included visits to various military training establishments and key ELT contacts in Kinshasa, winding up with a lunch with various key military personnel at the Embassy on the final Friday, then a visit to the radio station, before being driven to the airport to catch my flight back to Johannesburg on the Saturday morning.

We had a busy week, visiting the Military Academy, various Language Schools, different sections of the Embassy and key players in English teaching. The Embassy lunch was a bit of a let-down as, at the last minute, the military officials they had invited had been refused permission to attend. So they rounded up various Embassy staff and a few other people able to come for lunch at short notice! Then in the afternoon I was interviewed at the radio station.

I had been told an Embassy driver would collect me at 0800 a.m. to drive me to the airport for the flight which was leaving at 1200 noon. We got there around 1000 a.m. but there was no sign of a South African Airways flight on the departures board. Nor did there appear to be anyone on the South African Airways desk. I found a helpful counter assistant from another airline to ask about the flight and showed her my ticket. After studying it closely she said, "This flight went yesterday!"

Then the penny dropped. The entire programme had been one day in arrears. I had arrived on Saturday, the day before it said in the programme, and I should have left on the Friday, the day before my flight was listed in the programme. I hurriedly rushed outside and found the Embassy driver, who had said he would wait a few minutes to make sure I was safely checked in. He said that, if we hurried, we could make it back to the Embassy's travel agent in the town centre before they closed for the weekend at 1.00 p.m. We got there in the nick of time and they managed to book me on an evening flight the next day. However, this meant I missed my onward flight to Gaborone, so I had to stay the night in Johannesburg at a hotel inside the airport. That was the last time I ever set off to an unknown destination without asking for precise details of where I would be staying!

A few months later, Angus decided he had had enough of the DRC, and we recruited a new PEP manager, Danny Whitehead, to take over. It was very encouraging when he told my line manager a few months later, "Paul conducted my orientation the week after I arrived in DRC. Paul's advice and counsel was very much appreciated; starting a new position, particularly in a country with no British Council office for support has been difficult, but Paul's visit and guidance have been invaluable. I was immediately made to feel part of the British Council, and was left with a clear picture of how PEP DRC - and my position - fitted into the bigger British Council picture. Paul's visit enabled a smooth transition between project managers, and I very much appreciated the leadership and direction that was provided during the orientation."

The Teaching Centre in Mozambique continued to keep

me awake at nights. The Manager went off on maternity leave for several months and when she returned she clearly struggled to scope with the financial aspects of her role. At one point the Manager resigned. A new one was recruited who stayed just six months then she also left. There was a hiatus in recruiting a new manager, so I agreed I would spend two months in Maputo as temporary Teaching Centre Manager until the new recruit arrived. This meant getting to grips with timetabling - something I had not done since my VSO days in Nigeria - and trying to ensure that the books would balance.

By the end of the financial year the Teaching Centre had had five different people running it over the course of twelve months, and though it appeared on course to make a modest surplus, it ended the financial year £4000 in the red. This was used as an excuse to beat me over the head with in the annual performance assessment - something I found quite de-motivating, as I felt that rather than being marked down, I should have been complimented for keeping the show on the road, despite all the staff changes!

One of the highlights of my time in Botswana was a visit by Prince Harry. At the time he was linked romantically with Chelsy Davy. We had been warned by the Embassy to avoid any mention of Harry's night-time visit to The Bull and Bush on social media. The Botswana Sunday Standard reported,

"As part of the British royalty's activities during their visit to Botswana Prince Harry will officially launch the 2010 British Council Reading Challenge at one of the local primary schools. This year's reading challenge will be rolled out to 8 schools under the theme "Space Hop". The British Council will supply books for both young learners and older primary school pupils. The books will be mainly on space travel, and will be selected based on quality of writing and appeal to children. British Council Botswana Director Paul Woods said the aim of the challenge is to create a love of reading, support English language development, and encourage parents to get involved in their children's English language learning. Woods said Prince Harry will watch a display of traditional and modern dancing and then chat to pupils. Pupils will keep a record of the books they have read and all those who succeed in reading six books over a specified period will receive a medal in reward. "Like athletes in training, new readers need encouragement to grow in confidence," said Woods. The medal system breaks the Reading Challenge up into achievable goals for young readers.

Research has shown that children who took part in the challenge during their school holidays returned to school energized and eager to learn, often with a renewed enthusiasm for reading and all the advantages it offers. The Reading Challenge, which began as a UK initiative, is now run by 96% of British primary schools during the long summer holiday, with 700,000 children taking part. Woods said the British Council has now extended the programme to 23 different countries, including Botswana. The schools for the pilot project were selected with the help of the Ministry of Education and Skills Development. Prince Harry will be in Botswana from June 14-18, 2010."[72]

Each of the classes in the school had arranged a

display in honour of the Prince's visit. One of the groups had a cardboard box with a roll of paper which could be scrolled down in the opening for the tv screen, with a label on top saying "Chelsy Davy TV". There was some criticism in the local press that scantily clad school children had been lined up at 8.00 a.m. in the sunny but freezing cold weather to dance for Harry when he arrived at the school, where he was greeted by the 1000 or so pupils waving Botswana and Union Jack flags. He was later presented with a traditional African chair.

Ben Fogle reported in the Daily Mail when Prince William caught up with Harry the following day and they went cheetah petting at the Mokolodi Game Reserve:

"The boys arrive in a cavalcade of black BMWs. William and Harry pose with two orphaned cheetahs. The game wardens had been worried that the flashbulbs would scare the cats, but they take it in their stride - much as the Princes do. How does a 27-year-old cope with hundreds of journalists, I ask? 'This is a bit excessive,' William admits. 'There aren't usually quite so many. But my life is not always like this... It is difficult, flitting between military life and public life. There's loads of things I need to keep track of.'

Next stop is Mokolodi, a nature reserve ...where William and Harry are presented with an 8ft African rock python. Gamely, the boys agree to pose with it around their necks. You'd never get their dad doing that,' notes one photographer. 'You take the head,' William says, passing it to his brother. 'It's really squiggly.' The snake sticks out its tongue and Harry slowly moves it back towards his brother's face. 'Whoa, whoa, whoa,' says William, 'don't point it at me.' He pulls his face back just before the snake pees all over his shoulder, to the amusement of the crowd. 'It must be very relaxed,' he jokes. The young Princes are then honoured by having two snakes named after them. 'You can have the common house snake as it's the same colour as your hair,' Harry is told. 'Big brother gets the python, little brother gets the common house.'

As we say goodbye, there is a herd of elephants grazing next to an acacia tree. William stares at them intently. A smile breaks across his face. 'This place will hold a special place in my heart for the rest of my life,' he says. 'Africa's the perfect place to come. The locals haven't a clue who I am and I love that.' "[73]

When I took James and Marie cheetah petting at Mokolodi, there were a couple of Israeli tourists who came along with the same guide. One of the Israelis was wearing a long woollen jumper and managed to get his sleeve tangled up with the cheetah's claw. The cheetah snarled angrily and took a swipe at him with the other claw. I had visions of him being mauled to death but fortunately after more snarling and growling from the cheetah he managed to extricate himself and we beat a hasty retreat.

The Royal Visit coincided with the official Queen's Birthday Party, at which the Ambassador, Prince Harry and I had to make short speeches. The band played God Save the Queen and the Botswana National Anthem, and Mophato, a group of Batswana dancers sponsored by the British Council, who were about to go off to perform in the UK at the Sage Theatre in Newcastle, gave a brief performance. According to the Mophato website, "In 2009, whilst working for the Botswana society for the Arts,

Jeremy Avis met dancer and choreographer Andrew Kola, who was just getting his dance theatre company Mophato, off the ground. World Cup fever was already spreading through Southern Africa and the idea for a joint production celebrating African football was born. Through the generosity of the British Council in Botswana and other sponsors, Mophato was able to fully realise the training potential of this project by enabling an intensive rehearsal period with dancer / choreographer Nuno Da Silva and the opportunity to travel to the UK to work with Luca Silvestrini and stage this unique performance at the Sage Gateshead."[74]

UK in Botswana reported on Facebook, "Coinciding with the 2010 world cup in South Africa, Goalmouth! is a new piece of music and dance written by UK-based Korasong Radio especially to launch the Botswana dance company, Mophato Dance Theatre, onto the international stage, and to provide them with the experience of high quality professional training and international performance. A dramatic celebration of multiculturalism, Goalmouth! was performed by massed amateur choirs and Anglo-Gambian band Korasong Radio, with Mophato taking centre stage.

A documentary film, funded by the British Council and shown on the Africa Channel, followed the progress of Goalmouth! from the arrival in Botswana of top dancer and choreographer Nuno Silva to train five members of Mophato through to the first performance of Goalmouth! on 29 June 2010 at the prestigious theatre complex, The Sage, in Gateshead, Newcastle-upon-Tyne. Funding for Mophato and Goalmouth! was sourced in Botswana by the Botswana Society for the Arts (BSA). Profits from the performance at The Sage and from future performances will contribute to the realisation of the Botswana National Arts Institute.[75]

In August 2009 a new Director took over. Tanya Dunne had a background in Libraries and Information Science and this was her first overseas posting with the British Council. Unfortunately there had recently been a triennial review which recommended various cost cutting exercises and Botswana was one of the countries which was going to be hardest hit, with the number of local staff likely to be cut by half, from fourteen to seven. Tanya was extremely unfortunate to be in the wrong place at the wrong time. The Batswana staff did not take kindly to the forthcoming cuts and basically mutinied, sending a letter to the Regional Director accusing Tanya of professional incompetence, regularly arriving late for work and various other unsubstantiated allegations. One weekend in April she threw a complete wobbly, announcing she couldn't take any more of this, and a couple of days later she was on the plane home. This put the British Council into something of a quandary. The solution the Regional Director came up with was to offer me the temporary post of Director Botswana, which I held for six months from April to October 2010.

My task was to reduce the number of staff from 14 to 7 and recruit a locally appointed Director, whilst at the same time keeping up the motivation levels of the staff who were staying on. We managed to negotiate quite generous severance terms for the staff whose posts were to be suppressed, and my impression was that all those who actually wanted to leave went and those who preferred to stay on managed to stay. I had a major problem with one member of staff, who had been recruited in a marketing role for his flamboyant extrovert style, and who in his spare time was the Youth Co-ordinator for the main opposition party, the Botswana Movement for Democracy. An article appeared in a local newspaper encouraging people who wanted to join the party's youth wing to phone a number which turned out to be his British Council mobile number. This went against the staff code of conduct, which specified no involvement by staff in local politics, by making it appear that the British Council (co-located with the Embassy) was supporting the opposition party. I got permission to access his e-mail account and to my horror discovered a substantial cache of emails sent to and from his official British Council email address which had nothing to do with the Council and everything to do with promoting the Botswana Movement for Democracy. Given our location within the walls of the Embassy it would have been highly embarrassing if this had got into the public realm. The Embassy wanted him to be summarily dismissed, but it seemed fairer to go through the British Council's somewhat drawn out disciplinary procedures. Sensibly, he got the message and resigned before things escalated any further.

Another headache was the Director's accommodation. Our lease in Broadhurst was about to expire around the time that Tanya left, so we made plans to move to the Director's house, which was literally next door to the Presidential Palace, with a large and well-maintained garden and an attractive swimming pool with covered patio area which was ideal for barbecues. There were even three gas heaters by the pool for when it was cold at night in the Botswana winter! Tanya's predecessor had spent a fortune on getting the house upgraded with a new kitchen, new bathrooms and complete re-decoration throughout. However, the British Council's Global Estates Department had subsequently re-valued the upgraded accommodation from £500,000 to over £3 million. The increase in value was to be depreciated over the next few years and this made a very substantial hole in the annual country budget. I queried with London how the value could possibly have gone up so much after renovations costing around £300,000 at the most, but all I got from them was, "That's its current market value."

A few weeks later I had a good look round the Deputy High Commissioner's residence which was a couple of doors further down the road and seemed to be fairly comparable in size and state of repair to ours. He told me it was valued by the Foreign Office at around £600,000. So I wrote again to Global Estates saying could they check their records carefully as I was sure there must have been a mistake somewhere. Several weeks later I got a reply saying they had looked again in detail at the surveyor's report and there did seem to be a problem as the person doing the valuation had confused Botswana Pula and US dollars, so the actual revised value of the property should have been £600,000, rather than £3 million! We had had a substantial sum deducted from our budget the previous year to cover the supposedly increased valuation, so I asked if we could claw this back, but was told that because it had been deducted in the previous financial year it was now too late. It was water under the bridge and they couldn't do anything about it. However, they would amend the amount being charged to the Botswana budget for depreciation in the current year, which gave us a substantial windfall to spend. But it was not all good news, as along with the move to a locally-appointed successor, I was ordered to make plans to rent out the Director's house following our departure, in advance of it later being sold at the going market price.

The only downside to living next door to the presidential palace seemed to be that on the odd occasion when we had a noisy reception with loud music, we had to turn the volume down after 10 o'clock to avoid a knock on the door from a presidential guard to say that we were keeping the President awake.

The children came out two or three times a year. During the long summer holiday we decided it was time that James learnt to drive. However, when he applied for a Botswana learner's permit, he was told that, because he did not have a residence permit, but only a tourist visa, they could not issue him with a licence. Fanta found a way round this by getting him a Guinea licence, plus an international driving permit on the strength of the Guinea licence, which then allowed him to drive in Botswana as a qualified driver. We spent quite a lot of time practising the basics off-road behind our house. Then when we set off for a 2500 km road trip across the Kalahari Desert to Swakopmund on the coast of Namibia, James drove the car most of the way. The first time we came to a road block I was a bit apprehensive, but the police happily accepted his international driving licence as valid and on we went. There was hardly anything on the roads - at most another vehicle came in the opposite direction every half hour or so, and the only other hazards were the odd cow or goat sitting in the middle of the road.

One of the highlights of this trip was staying in some typical Kalahari bushmen's huts at Ghanzi Trailblazers. This was a former cattle ranch where the owners had recreated a typical San bushman community. The only concession to civilisation was that the rustic huts had proper beds and mosquito nets, showers heated by a "donkey" boiler, and a small bar. Nearby there was an abandoned quarry with deep water ideal for swimming and diving, and at night the local bushmen entertained guests with traditional songs and dancing far into the night.

From here we carried on to Windhoek, the capital of Namibia, where the Council Director Ronnie Micallef, who was away on leave, had kindly allowed us to stay in their house. We spent a couple of days exploring the sights of Windhoek, including the Botanical Gardens, before setting off on the long journey to the coast at Swakopmund. Here we slummed it for a couple of nights in Villa Wiese, a cheap backpackers lodge, before treating ourselves to luxury accommodation at The Stiltz. As one satisfied guest here wrote, "Stiltz is truly enchanting, with its gorgeous bungalows atop stilts surrounded by trees and desert plants. Flamingos and pelicans can be seen flying past, the ocean is within easy walking distance, and the comfy furnishings seem designed for maximum relaxation. A central gazebo outfitted with plush sofas has marvellous ocean views, as does the breakfast hall... The beds were exceptionally comfortable and we slept soundly and deeply. The charming and friendly staff placed paw-paw (papaya) in a nearby tree to attract several species of birds, making this an unforgettable breakfast! Wandering around the property we were delighted to find a dozen camels chewing on tall grasses close to the ocean."[76]

One of the highlights was visiting Dune 7 near Walvis Bay. Said to be the highest sand dune in Namibia, the views from the top are spectacular and sand boarding down is an exhilarating, if potentially dangerous, experience. James managed a complete wipe-out and tumbled head over heels several times before coming to rest upside down.

On New Year's Eve, we had supper with Sten and Anna-Carin Stenbeck and their family who we had met by chance (we knew them from the Hash in Gaborone) and lit some sparklers with their children before adjourning to the beach to see in the new year, where there was an enormous bonfire about fifty feet high, potentially extremely dangerous. At one point it toppled over, showering sparks in all directions and narrowly missing the crowds of people gathered around it.

We got safely back to the outskirts of Gaborone, after several quite severe rainstorms in the Kalahari, and with James driving most of the way. We had literally reached a few hundred yards from our house when the engine stopped and the car wouldn't start. We had prayed for a safe journey and indeed our prayers were answered! It turned out to be a problem with the starter motor which needed replacing. We truly breathed a sigh of relief that we had broken down so close to home and not in the middle of the Kalahari desert!

During one run with the Hash running club, I took a lengthy short cut through some long grass. A few days later I developed a very stiff neck and felt distinctly ill with fever, a headache and joint pains. The doctor diagnosed tick bite fever and prescribed doxycycline, which seemed to work after a few days. That was the last time I would take a short cut through long grass in Botswana!

By May 2008 I was starting to get itchy feet. I wrote to our old friend Peter Arnstein from Canbury Park Church:

"Dear Peter, It's been some time since we were in contact - here's a quick update. Fanta is still in Guinea doing battle with the president's wife. Please carry on praying for a just and speedy resolution! I am contemplating retiring 18 months early from the British Council and moving to Mozambique to work for Danida in Tete Province. I will have an interview from 9-12 June in Copenhagen. Fanta is not keen as Tete is very remote - but they pay boarding school fees and by retiring I would be able to pay off the mortgage and then earn enough over the next few years to pay off credit card and other debts before retiring properly when Marie goes to university. Please pray that God will guide us to where he wants us to be!"

At the end of May I wrote, "Dear Ralph and Lan, Fanta seems to be not the only one trying to prise money out of the Guinea presidency - the army has mutinied and on Thursday she got stuck in the centre of town because rebel soldiers and troops loyal to the president Lansana Conteh were taking pots shots at each other and the presidential guard had sealed off all the roads. The Americans seem to be interfering - on Wednesday the mutineers stopped a US military plane from landing at Conakry airport, and they still seem to be holding the second in command of the army hostage until they get their demands met!"

DANIDA paid all the expenses for a five-day trip to Copenhagen, including three nights in a very pleasant hotel close to the centre. The interviews were spread over a couple of days, with a Portuguese language test and psychological test on the first day, then a group selection board and final interview for the three preferred candidates on the second day. I had taken a 500-page report in Portuguese (I couldn't find an English version) and ploughed through this in between going to see the Little Mermaid, sampling pickled herring and doing various other touristy things the day after I arrived while I was still jet-lagged.

A few weeks later I wrote to one of the other candidates to whom I had been chatting prior to the final interview:

"Dear Ingrid,

You may remember we met as you were on the way out from your interview in Copenhagen and I was on the way in. Did you get the job - if so, hearty congratulations! I thought I did ok in the interview but was a bit surprised to discover only a few minutes earlier that it was all going to be in Portuguese, especially as we'd had a two-hour Portuguese test the day before! I also found it a bit strange that they had paid for me to come all the way to Denmark only for the final interview to be a teleconference in Portuguese with a panel at the Danish Embassy in Maputo. As I'm working here in Maputo at the moment, I could have just gone down the road and met them face-to-face! I guess my consolation prize was that a few days later our Teaching Centre Manager in Maputo resigned at short notice so I will be spending the next few weeks in Mozambique as Acting Teaching Centre

Manager whilst we recruit a replacement. This made me realise that life in Tete would probably have been pretty difficult, so I wasn't really too disappointed that I didn't get offered the job. If you didn't get the Tete job and are still in Luanda, do stay in touch and we'll have a beer or two the next time I visit Angola!"

I did in fact make it to Angola the following February, killing several birds with one stone, checking on the progress of the Peacekeeping English Project there, managed by Chris Lawrence who I knew well from Latvia, and exploring the options for setting up a revenue earning Direct Teaching of English Centre with an Angolan partner. At the same time I was able to visit most of our key ELT contacts in Luanda. En route to Angola from London I had to change planes in Johannesburg. When I had checked in at the airport, I was intending to check my baggage just to Joburg, then collect it and re-check it to Luanda. However, the check-in clerk was too quick off the mark and checked it straight through to Luanda. When I objected, she got quite stroppy, so I just said, "OK then, I just hope it gets through Joburg airport safely," and thought no more of it. When I arrived in Luanda there was no sign of the checked baggage, and the next BA flight wasn't until four days later. I asked the Defence Attache if his driver could take me shopping to buy some shirts and trousers. "You'll be lucky", he said. "There's nowhere here where you can buy formal western clothes." There was a market where you could buy second-hand clothing which I got the driver to take me to, but the only shirts they had were t-shirts with slogans on them. Not the kind of thing you could wear to go and see the Minister of Education. Fortunately the Defence Attache was roughly the same size and shape as me, so I got by with borrowing a couple of shirts and a pair of trousers from him, which kept me going until my suitcase arrived four days later.

Meanwhile I carried on applying for other posts including one based in Kenya, but didn't even get shortlisted. A few years earlier, I had been part of a small group at Hitchin where the British Council was sending batches of thirty or so current or prospective country directors and managers on a very intensive course designed to break people down and get them to comply with the corporate direction which the British Council at the time under David Greene thought they should follow. (This was around the same time that the Council was encouraging people to attend highly suspect courses organised by "Common Purpose", which were intended to create masonic-like cabals within the civil service, police and other government departments). According to the conspiracy theory website "Common Purpose Exposed": [77]

"Common Purpose (CP) is a Charity, based in Great Britain, which creates 'Future Leaders' of society. CP selects individuals and 'trains' them to learn how society works, who 'pulls the levers of power' and how CP 'graduates' can use this knowledge to lead 'Outside Authority'. But evidence shows that Common Purpose is rather more than a Charity 'empowering' people and communities'. In fact, CP is an elitist pro-EU political organisation helping to replace democracy in UK, and worldwide, with CP-chosen 'elite' leaders. In truth, their hidden networks and political objectives are undermining and destroying our democratic society and are threatening 'free will' in adults, teenagers and children.

Their work is funded by public money and big business, including international banks. Using behavioural programming and experiential learning techniques, the views of graduates can be remoulded to conform to the new Common Purpose. Most will not be aware this has happened, but we are given immediate clues in descriptions by graduates that Common Purpose training is 'life changing', 'disturbing', or 'unsettling'. Trained and operating under the Chatham House rules of secrecy (details of discussion, those present and location are not disclosed), CP graduates come to operate in 'their world' of Common Purpose."

Several people including experienced Country Directors couldn't take the strain and cracked under the pressure of being neuro-linguistically programmed on the Hitchin course. In January 2009 I had written to James Kennedy who had been part of my small sub-group at Hitchin, where we had bared our souls to each other, and thus created a common and lasting bond:

"My post here as English Manager Sub-Saharan Africa based in Botswana ends next September. I applied for a similar post in Band 8 in Nairobi just before Christmas and was rather taken aback not even to be shortlisted - but consoled my wounded self-esteem with the thought that this probably says more about the corrupt nature of the Council's selection processes in the former East and West Africa region than about my own abilities and skills! But it's a bit worrying that one of the people who didn't even shortlist me is now my new line manager!

James, now 18 has just finished his first term doing Biology at Leeds. Marie now 14 is doing well at The Leys School in Cambridge. If it wasn't for the fact that the

Council is paying her boarding school fees, I'd be thinking of retiring next year, but as it is, I'm going to have to soldier on for another few years yet before I can go off and do the things I 've always really wanted to do! They were both here for Christmas and we had a great trip to the Chobe Game Park in the far north of Botswana, plus a day going to see Victoria Falls. The last time I went there was when I was in Tanzania in 1980, about 3 weeks after Rhodesia became Zimbabwe, when it felt like going to Paradise! It's somewhat ironical that Mugabe has managed to totally wreck the economy and Zimbabweans now have to go to Tanzania and other nearby countries to get basic commodities, as there's absolutely nothing in the shops in Zimbabwe, and a 10 million zim dollar bill isn't enough to buy a loaf of bread! [It was to get worse - by mid 2015 the Wall St Journal reported that a 100 trillion zim dollar bill was worth a mere 40 US cents!]

Fanta is still doing battle with what is now (as of last week) the ex-regime in Guinea. A court in Conakry awarded her a large sum in damages after the President's wife occupied our house in Conakry for several years and the presidential guards this woman installed there completely trashed it. But the Central Bank has so far failed to pay up! Fanta is flying there on Sunday to see if she can make any headway now that Lansana Conte has died and an army captain, Dadis Camara, has taken over in a military coup, promising to stamp out graft and corruption. We shall see...."

At the same time I wrote to the Editor of Private Eye "Dear Lord Gnome

Following the death of Lansana Conte, (the ageing general who had ruled the west African state of Guinea for 25 years and managed to reduce what, as the world's largest producer of bauxite, should be one of the most prosperous countries in Africa, to one of the poorest and most corrupt), it would be good if Private Eye could run a "Letter from Conakry" feature, summarising recent events and expressing some hope for the future. Guinea was second only to Haiti last year as Transparency International's most corrupt country on earth and during a general strike last year over 150 people were killed in a little reported street protest against the grinding poverty to which Conte had reduced the country. Captain Dadis Camara, the young soldier who has taken command and sacked at least some of the old guard of Conte cronies who were running the country, needs all the support he can get to turn the country round, restore democracy and human rights and root out bribery, nepotism and corruption. The attitude of the US government, which in response to the coup has cut off aid to Guinea, is particularly unhelpful.

I confess to a personal interest, as my wife's house in Conakry was commandeered three years ago by Henriette, the former president's first wife, who installed a posse of presidential guards (colloquially known as red caps) in the property. Over the next two years they managed to trash the place completely. After a lengthy court case, the court awarded substantial compensation to my wife last year, but Madame Conte refused to accept the court's authority and installed a Catholic priest as a squatter in the property. Since Conte died on 23 December my wife has gone off to Guinea to see if, under the new regime, she can obtain some redress.

One is reminded of the biblical story of Naboth, in

which the evil Jezebel egged on her husband Ahab to get rid of Naboth and commandeer his vineyard, but was denounced by the Prophet Elijah and thrown out of a window, ending up dead in the street below, with the dogs licking her blood. One would not wish a similar fate on Henriette Conte, but it is to be hoped that Captain Camara's new regime will turn the country around, enforce the rule of law and stamp out the endemic graft and corruption which characterised Guinea under the Conte regime. If you don't plan to run an article on Guinea, I don't mind you printing this as a reader's letter, but under the pseudonym 'vengeanceismine.'"

At the same time I wrote to the US Ambassador in Conakry,

"Your Excellency

It is deplorable that the US has cut off aid to Guinea at a time when the recently installed regime of Captain Camara offers at least the hope of a return to democracy, respect for human rights and the rule of law in Guinea. With respect, if the US is hoping to support a return to power by the cronies and generals who surrounded Lansana Conte and his first wife Henriette, you are backing the wrong side.

It is only since Captain Camara's new regime took power that we have succeeded in regaining possession of our house in Nongo, which was illegally commandeered by Henriette Conte 3 years ago. Despite a legal judgement in our favour last year, she had ignored the court's ruling and continued to occupy the house, installing a Catholic priest as a squatter. However this week we finally managed to get this man and the presidential guards who had been illegally occupying the house out and regained possession of the building. It is therefore disappointing that the US appears in the eyes of the world to be backing the supporters of the corrupt and nepotistic former regime which rode roughshod over human rights and the property rights of individuals.

I should be grateful if you could pass these views on to the Guinea desk in the State Department."

The Ambassador did not deign to reply.

Early in January I wrote to the Grand Master of the Kathmandu hash, David "Rotter" Potter:

"New year's greetings from Botswana. Here, where the highest mountain in the country is about 1500 feet above sea level, I feel definite "saudades" (an untranslatable Portuguese word meaning something like nostalgia) for Nepal. Next week's hash in Gaborone is at the Lion Park - though we are assured that all the lions which might have gone for slow moving runners or walkers have died.... Usually the temperature here is around 35 degrees C which is not conducive to over-exercising, so hashes are either short and sweet on Mondays at 6 p.m. or more laid back and leisurely on Sundays at 10 a.m. followed by a barbeque lunch. I am building up a reputation for laying runs which are long and devious with lots of back checks but when anyone complains the run took more than an hour I remind them that if they were in Nepal the walk would be at least two hours and the run the same or longer.... Some hashers are just not serious!
Best wishes for 2009
Victim"

Around this time I put in for the Band 8 2010 overseas

deployment exercise which seemed like my last chance to get another overseas post with the Council before compulsory retirement kicked in at sixty. My Line Manager was less than flattering in his comments on team management - "English in Sub Saharan Africa does not have quite the same sense of team as exams and Teaching Centres. Those managing English are a diverse group of some English specialists (Nigeria and Sudan) and some general business managers." Nor were his comments on building relationships particularly glowing, "Paul is trying hard to find a sponsor for the radio initiative, and that effort is worth recognising even though it has yet to produce a result. Paul continues to work at important internal relationships. He has won credit in London with his enthusiasm and determination to make Global English work, but has not yet been able to steer stakeholders for English to endorse the strategy he put together in the early part of the year, and is now contributing to the team working on a holistic English strategy for the region." Not surprisingly in view of these less than helpful comments I did not succeed in getting a post overseas in 2010.

I wrote to Nigel Wakeham, the architect who had designed our ill-fated house in Conakry:

"We've been in Botswana now for the past two and a half years but they're just about to abolish my post - they prefer using consultants like Joy Griffiths who cost a lot more per day but may be cheaper in the long run than permanent staff. I'm hoping to hang in there for a few more years at least till Marie has finished her GCSEs next year - she's at a boarding school in Cambridge. James is now taking re-sits. Fanta is back in Guinea again, fighting a lengthy court case against the ex-president's wife trying to get compensation for her having trashed our house. It's starting to look reasonably promising - the court has apparently ordered some of her assets should be auctioned off to pay the compensation. Fanta's also trying to sell the trashed house, though in its dilapidated state it's not worth very much! If we do get at least some of the money she is claiming off the ex-president's wife, she'll probably have to stay there and do the place up, as it would then be much more saleable. Quite a saga!!

Ralph and Lan Stather came out for a two-week visit in March. I took a couple of long weekends off so I could accompany them on trips to the Okavango Delta and Maun.

By August 2010 I was starting to get a bit desperate, when they offered me a job in Manchester. I wrote to Ralph and Lan,

"Good to hear all your news. I've got a British Council job to go to in Manchester from early October. The job title - Account Coordinator - doesn't exactly inspire me but it would pay Marie's school fees for another three years (unless they change the rules, which seems quite likely!)

But I flew to London last week for an interview for an English Project Manager post with the BBC World Service Trust in Bangladesh. Now waiting to hear the result. There's a 50 /50 chance, as they were only interviewing me and one other person. The job sounds very interesting but Fanta is not thrilled by the prospect of living in Dhaka. She is on her way back from Guinea having finally sold her house. She got waylaid at Conakry airport with a large amount of dollars and was told to go back and get some other papers or they would confiscate it under anti-trafficking laws when she tried to pay it into a bank anywhere in the EU.

Anyway, if the dosh ever gets to where it needs to go, we should be able to pay off our substantial debts and the mortgage and if Marie wasn't in the boarding school I could retire. So a few major decisions are looming....Will let you know where we end up."

I came second. I heard on the grapevine that the BBC made an internal appointment, which suggested they might have just been going through the motions of recruiting externally.

8 MANCHESTER

A few weeks before Christmas we moved back to Chester and I began my new job as Account Coordinator for the Education UK website. The job was described as being to "manage all aspects of the Education UK website including contracts management, liaising with contractors and suppliers, and improving the technical functionality delivered by the project."

Anyone who has worked for the Council in English teaching will probably be familiar with David Blackie's Blog. This amply identified, over the course of more than a decade, various shortcomings in the Council's management of transparent tendering, competent web design and fair treatment of competitors.

What I inherited was a website which did not function as it was supposed to; there were sub-contracts with five suppliers: Sapient to do the web design and functionality; Hotcourses (a firm set up by Jeremy Hunt and Mike Elms which ran a rival website) to sell advertising space and manage the non-tertiary level data feed; and the Guardian creating content. It was a total nightmare. The contracts had been due for extension/renewal shortly before I arrived in Manchester. There had been a competitive tendering exercise and the marking team had initially awarded the contract for selling space on the website to a firm called Sunguard. Then for some unexplained reason, the panel which had been scoring the bids was dismissed and then re-convened with different members who subsequently awarded the contract to Hotcourses.

I wrote to an old friend from Oxford:
"We've been back in Chester for 6 weeks now and I'm working for British Council in Manchester managing the Education UK website (which is another story). It's a real dog's breakfast – the company which they appointed to market the site then set up its own competing website – something which was not precluded in their contract and so this was perfectly legal, although perhaps morally questionable."

Jeremy Hunt had appeared in The New Statesman's list of potential rivals to David Cameron:
"Jeremy Hunt, 42
` Shadow culture, media and sport secretary
Education Charterhouse School. Oxford University
Wealth £4.1m

Hunt is paid £1,000 a month for two hours of business advice to Hotcourses Ltd, an educational guide publisher, and enjoyed a £245,181 dividend payment from the company in 2006. He still felt hard-pressed enough to submit an invoice for 1p for a 12-second mobile phone call."[78]

There was more. According to the Mirror, which published a story under the headline 'Top Tory's windfalls as he sharpens axe':

"ConDem bigwig Jeremy Hunt has pocketed almost £2 million as he gets ready to slash jobs.

The multi-millionaire, 43, a key ally of David Cameron, led Tory attacks on "fat cats" before the election. But the Farnham MP will not feel the coming cuts thanks to a fortune estimated at £4.1million even before the latest payouts from Hotcourses where he has made his money. Mr Hunt owns almost 50% of the firm, entitling him to about half of the £2 million it paid out in dividends to its four shareholders last year. His 285,095 shares brought him another £885,000 this year, according to calculations based on the company's accounts. Mr Hunt's website reveals he now does no work for the company. It states: 'Since being elected as a Member of Parliament, Jeremy has stepped aside from all management responsibilities in the company'. A spokeswoman for Mr Hunt, who earns £134,565 a year as a Cabinet minister, said he did not wish to comment on the Hotcourses cash."[79]

According to a somewhat evasive reply to a Freedom of Information request put to the British Council in 2015, the Council at that time had one live three-year contract for the management of the Education UK website, signed on 23 July 2013.[80] Under this contract Hotcourses acted as an agent for the British Council via what was effectively a Partnership Agreement, rather than a Supplier Agreement. This meant that Hotcourses was responsible for selling advertising options to institutions across the Education UK website and related activities. Amounts varied depending on the success of the site and institution budgets/marketing needs, and therefore were not able to be specified in the contract. The service provided covered technical and commercial management of the Education UK website. The British Council did not pay Hotcourses for services relating to the Education UK website, but rather the build and maintenance of the Education UK website was funded by advertising contracts with participating institutions. Hotcourses received the income, took their costs from that income and the remaining funds were split 50-50.

Total payments to Hotcourses were:

2010/2011 = £219,669.05
2011/2012 = £270,832.61
2012/2013 = £228,296.98
2013/2014 = £96,820.00
2014/2015 = £249,500.23

In September 2013 the Guardian reported that Jeremy Hunt could stand to gain £17 million if the sale of Hotcourses to a company called Inflexion went through. "The proposed deal, valuing the whole company at about £35 m, would cement the health secretary's reputation as one of the most successful entrepreneurs in the House of Commons. Although Hunt stepped down as a director of Hotcourses in 2009, he is still the largest shareholder, with a 49% stake. His interest in the firm is held via a "blind trust" which means he is prevented from having any day to day control of his stake."[81] However this sale did not proceed.

In February 2016 the British Council announced, "The current services provided by Hotcourses Ltd will continue as usual for our customers and clients throughout 2016, ending on 31st January 2017. In February 2017, the British Council will launch a new non-commercial Education UK digital approach to provide objective information about UK Education. This new approach will provide a wide range of digital channels to reflect the strong global interest in the many aspects of UK Education from overseas governments and institutions, as well as potential students and their influencers, including education agents."[82]

Then in January 2017 the BBC reported that Hotcourses was being bought for £30 million by the Australian firm IDP Education. Hunt owned a 48% stake in Hotcourses, which was therefore valued at just over £14m. He said he would use the money to fund campaigns after he leaves politics. IDP Education said that it and the Hotcourses businesses would retain their identity and continue to operate separately, but would collaborate.[83] PIE News reported that the purchase would add some of the world's largest education search websites including Whatuni, The Complete University Guide and Hotcourses Abroad to the IDP Australia's portfolio.[84]

It seems that the Council had finally managed to extricate itself from the toxic relationship it had had with Hotcourses over the years. By selling out to IDP Australia, already the co-owner of the IELTS language test together with the Council and Cambridge Assessment, Hotcourses dealt the final blow to any aspirations the Council once had to make a commercial success of the Education UK website.

The rules on boarding school allowances stated in black and white, "If your children continue in boarding school when you transfer to the UK, the allowance may continue, provided you are expected to go overseas for your next job within five years of your return to the UK. Where this is not the case, payment will continue until the completion of the examination course already embarked on, for example, GCSE examinations." However, not long after our arrival back in the U.K., we got a letter from an over-zealous official in the British Council's HR department saying that, as I was now working in the UK, Marie's boarding school allowance would cease at the end of the summer term. This threatened to throw a cat amongst the pigeons as Marie was about to start her "A" levels and I was continuing to apply for posts overseas. If I succeeded, and we had had to move Marie to a state school in Chester, this would completely mess her around if we then had to send her back to the boarding school a few months later. All attempts to make HR see reason having failed, I launched a grievance against the Head of the Personnel Department. The school was very supportive, in fact they even offered to provide an additional bursary covering 50% of the fees.

I wrote to the bursars office,

"Dear Mrs Cooksey

Thank you so much for your letter of 4 February informing us that the committee is offering a 40% bursary in addition to Marie's 10% scholarship to enable her to complete her A levels at The Leys, which we would like to accept. This is a great relief at what has been quite a stressful time for us.

I have not yet heard the outcome of grievance which I launched internally against the Head of Personnel at the British Council. If this is unsuccessful, the PCS union is very likely to provide a lawyer to assist with a court case in the County Court for loss of earnings and also a parallel appeal to an industrial tribunal on the grounds of age discrimination. I also have an interview later this week for a post as Director Southern Sudan which, if I were to be successful, would automatically re-qualify me for Boarding School allowance for the duration of the posting, so the problem would go away.

I am fairly confident that, one way or another, although it could take quite a long time, we will win! I will of course let you know if my employers have a change of heart or, failing that, if we are successful in either of the legal cases which would then ensue."

The PCS Union was extremely supportive, and the Council, realising it was unlikely to win if the case went to court, backed down a couple of months later. I wrote to some friends,

"Praise God! Our prayers have been answered - the British Council has reversed its earlier decision to stop paying Marie's school fees at the end of next term, and has now agreed to keep on paying the fees till she completes her A levels in summer 2013! This means she can stay on at the Leas School in Cambridge, where she is very happy, is doing well, both in sport and academically, and has loads of good friends."

Meanwhile, at work, David Blackie continued to point out the shortcomings of the Education UK website. Officially I could not comment, but I did feel considerable sympathy for the way he had been treated by the Council, and although I couldn't admit it publicly, a lot of what he said was pretty accurate.

His blog noted:

"Education UK - the second most used resource after Google. By prospective international students, that is. That's what the British Council says on its own site about Education UK - see for yourself what they say about the site development and management. If what they say is true about numbers using their site, it really is a chronic problem for UK education. To be on this site British educational institutions pay from £500 for a bog-standard page for a language school to an eye-watering £4550 for an interactive "rich" record (whatever that might be) for a college or university.

We have produced two reports showing the results of searches on the site - and anybody can verify the reports' findings. The main one covers all course categories (A levels, Degrees, Research etc.) with select subject area (Computing, Business, Engineering etc.) search results, and the second is a shorter report which focuses purely on English language course searches. Responses to the findings in my inbox say "diabolical", "a farce", "astonishing", "it beggars belief".

The British Council was first told their site didn't work when it went up in January 2002. It never worked and today, nine years after launch and almost a year after introducing a "completely new" version of the site, it still doesn't."[85]

Other bloggers joined in the chorus, including John Ward of 'The Slog', who in a series of blog posts entitled Hunt Balls, which were hard-hitting but a bit short on concrete facts, questioned Jeremy Hunt's very special relationship with the British Council.[86]

In the Spring of 2011 I drafted a short article entitled, 'Oh I Do Like To Be Beside The Seaside' for *IATEFL Selections* about the annual conference I had just attended in Brighton,[87]

"Brighton 2011 was a tremendously stimulating experience for me in three distinct areas: innovation, networking and entertainment. Ever since last October, when the British Council deployed me to Manchester - to a job which has nothing whatsoever to do with ELT - I have felt there must be more to life and work than the Education UK website....

Innovation – Staying at the Cutting Edge

Brighton provided an opportunity to stay abreast of cutting edge developments especially in technology and digital products/applications. The highlights for me were Steve Bukin's talk on *The Futurology of EFL*, where he painted a picture of what the ELT landscape might look like in 20-30 years' time, in a world where voice recognition and production technology has been perfected and robot teachers (already being used in Korea and Japan to teleport teachers from the Philippines) may make us all redundant. A talk by Michael Carrier on *Handheld Learning* (repeated the next day at the British Council reception) summarised a whole range of innovations using digital technology, whilst a fascinating account by Raquel D'Oliviera from the Rio Cultura Inglesa - with the intriguing title *CULTWEEPLE* - demonstrated how tweeting can be a hugely motivating factor in encouraging students to write (we even learned that Twibes can cater for closed groups and postings longer than 150 words!). Graham Stanley's session on *Digital Play* was quite an eye-opener on how to make use of gaming as a teaching tool, cashing in on students' fascination with this as a pastime and the huge levels of motivation it can generate. The result of the IATEFL/ELT Journal Debate on the motion *"Tweeting is for the birds, not language learning"* was pretty much a foregone conclusion, with Alan Waters shooting himself in the foot defending the motion against Nicky Hockly, who had technology and most of the audience on her side, not to mention live tweets appearing on the screen in real time from her supporters dotted around the room. Many of the contributions from the floor revolved around multi-tasking, with one contributor saying this was the best such debate ever. Gavin Dudeney's presentation *"Location, Location, Location: mLearning in Practice"* was a triumph of form over content, with a brilliantly crafted Powerpoint presentation including strangely bubble-like transitions demonstrating how various applications could be blended into classroom teaching, while Graeme Hodgson's case study on e-English for teachers demonstrated how an e-training course was delivered to public school teachers in Latin American schools in a highly cost-effective manner. I left the conference convinced it was time to throw away my old mobile and join the 21st century with at least an I-pad or I-phone for my next birthday – especially after sitting next to Gary Motteram in a session where we were encouraged to discuss with our neighbour what digital devices we owned and feeling quite embarrassed when he reeled off a list of at least 20 devices, including several I had never even heard of, when the most I could manage myself was a couple of mobiles, a laptop, a digital camera and a flip video. I was stunned by Sue Palmer's plenary talk on toxic pitfalls in child development - (which I was able to watch, via IATEFL Online, lying in bed before breakfast the next morning in the comfort of my hotel room, having spent the Sunday morning celebrating Palm Sunday at the local Baptist church). Later that day I found myself sitting on the sea wall counting the number of pushchairs going past below with babies facing the wrong way - 20 out of 25 - and trying hard to resist the urge to rush up to their mothers and ask, "Do you realise your baby's pushchair is retarding its language development?"

Networking – Old and New Friendships

IATEFL conferences are a great opportunity for networking, with old friends from way back, with current British Council colleagues and also for making new friends who share a common interest in different aspects of ELT. Some of the most thought-provoking sessions were given by delegates from Africa and Hornby scholars from other regions who are struggling to teach and train teachers with very few resources and very large classes, and I thought it was a great idea to raise funds for the WMIS scheme (which provides free memberships for teachers in Africa where there is no IATEFL affiliate) by selling attractive lapel badges.

Entertainment

Now that I qualify for my free bus pass, the old adage "all work and no play makes Jack a dull boy" is becoming increasingly meaningful. And indeed there was plenty of entertainment on offer. As the guidebook in the hotel warned, "with the historic Lanes, over 400 restaurants, and the sparkling nightlife, the only commodity in short supply will be time". Before the conference had even got under way, I had managed to get a ticket to see Patty Griffiths from BEBC/Kingdom Enterprises starring in *"Time and the Conways"* at the cosy Little Theatre. On Saturday night Macmillan had invited everyone at the conference to celebrate *Ten Years of One Stop English* at the Honey Club to the sounds of Rock 'n Roll from an Elvis look-alike. With considerable effort I dragged myself away from this event in time to catch *Regency Revels* with Mark Fletcher where we all joined in a raucous version of "Oh I do like to be beside the seaside" (the lady next to me produced some really authentic seagull sounds), every group was a winner in the quiz, and we all went away with a piece of authentic Brighton rock. This song also figured in *"An evening with Mrs Hooper"*, a fiendishly funny satire featuring a Brighton landlady who took in overseas students, taught them about tea and biscuits and had quite outspoken and very un-PC views on almost everything, including how not to give a presentation using "Walter's" notes. I squeezed in a visit to the Museum which had a fascinating local history section devoted to the more exotic side of Brighton life (including naughty postcards, dirty weekends, and more recently, Gay Pride marches). And what a delight to attend sessions in the Old Ship Hotel, especially in the room with chandeliers and tapestry wallpaper where Paganini the great violinist once played in December 1831.

I left Brighton with a long list of books to buy, a sense of fulfilment at having managed to upload the presentations from the *English in Africa* symposium to the IATEFL Online website, a renewed determination to step up my efforts to get back into ELT, and a note in my diary to keep the dates free for next year's conference."[87]

A few months later I wrote to Peter Arnstein:

"Fanta is very close to resolving things in Guinea (where she has been trying to get compensation from the ex-President's wife for having trashed the house we used to own there for several years now). She came back here briefly for Christmas then returned to Guinea where she has been ever since! The bailiff has now extracted some of the money owed to us from the lady's bank account and paid it into Fanta's local account in Guinea. Now all that remains is to extract this from the Guinea bank and move it to the UK (though this seems to be not entirely straightforward!). This has been a long-drawn out and quite stressful process, so we will be really glad when it's all over.

I'm soldiering on with managing the British Council's Education UK website (also not very straightforward - the firm contracted to do the marketing is owned by Jeremy Hunt, now the Minister of Culture, and no sooner had his firm been awarded the contract a year ago than they set up their own competing website!) I've still got itchy feet and am currently applying for a post as English Manager for Latin America, based in Argentina, but, now that I qualify for my bus pass, it's getting increasingly difficult competing against much younger "high-fliers", even when they don't have very much experience."

I didn't feel quite so bad about all the problems with the Education UK website when I read about the problems the Equality and Human Rights Commission had been having with its website in the Guardian for 21 June 2011: "The commission spent £874,000 on a website which experienced serious technical difficulties and decided to write off its losses, but did not get the ministerial approval that is needed for losses of more than £100,000."[88]

In August 2011 two British teachers were locked in a cellar at the British Council office in Kabul during an 8-hour shootout with the Taliban in which 12 people were killed. One of them had only arrived in Afghanistan two days earlier, the other, from South Africa, used to be a teacher at the British Council in Mozambique when I was in charge of the Teaching Centre there, and then subsequently managed the Mozambique Peacekeeping English Project before moving on to teaching English and training teachers in Afghanistan.

Nicole Janneker wrote, "I'm ok. It was awful but we will all be fine. I'm in London for treatment at the moment. Will be going to South Africa for a short time at the end of the week and hoping to return to Kabul by mid-September to restart our programmes and show our continued support to all our Afghan colleagues and partners who have been most adversely affected by this. Thank you for getting in touch and for keeping us in your thoughts and prayers. It is truly a miracle that we are alive to tell the tale."

The following month I got some really good news. I wrote to friends at Kingsway Chapel:

"A big thank you to all those who were praying about my job interview last Friday. I went into the interview knowing that people were praying and it really made a big difference! I'd had several other job interviews recently but kept quiet about them. This time I felt much more confident and relaxed, knowing that you were supporting me in prayer!

I just had a phone call from the recruiting manager in Argentina to say that they are offering me the job (as English Advisor for the southern half of Latin America, based in Buenos Aires). There are still a few bureaucratic hoops to jump through yet (e.g. medicals), but the expectation is that we will be leaving Chester at the end of August/beginning of September, and will be in Buenos Aires for the next 2-3 years. It will be a pity to leave you folks just when we are starting to know you better, but we're very grateful for all your help, guidance and fellowship over the past six months since we arrived back from Botswana."

9 ARGENTINA

In early October we moved to Argentina. On our arrival we were put up in an empty flat belonging to the Embassy in the Belgrano area of Buenos Aires, which gave us time to look around in a leisurely fashion for somewhere more permanent. It was a short one-stop fifteen-minute ride on the ancient train from Belgrano to Retiro station, then a five minute walk up the hill to the British Council office.

A couple of days after arriving, I was thrown in at the deep end, on a plane to the annual FAAPI English Teachers' Conference in Salta. This was an excellent opportunity to meet all the key players in English teaching throughout the country. My job was entitled "English Adviser for the Southern Cone", i.e. Argentina, Chile, Uruguay and Paraguay. Quite what I was supposed to do on a tiny grant budget of around £50,000 per year was not very clearly spelled out - it was up to me to secure contributions from partners and to find ways and means of earning some revenue.

A few weeks after our arrival, we found out about a project being put out to tender in Uruguay. I wrote to an old friend who was now working for the Open University in Bangladesh,

"Hi Mike,

We just found out over the weekend about a very interesting Invitation to Bid for a project with Plan Ceibal in Uruguay which was being tracked for some time by British Council, then all went quiet. The ITB was issued on 15 November with a deadline for submission of 15 December. I imagine the Open University will have also been interested in bidding and may have had much better intelligence than we did! Can you find out who we need to contact in the OU to see if they might be interested in joining forces (with the BC in a subordinate role?). We have quite a lot of relevant materials, e.g. for the teacher training and online materials elements of the project but with only 5 working days to the deadline we would find it logistically impossible to put in a bid of our own at this very late stage in the proceedings. But we could join forces and thus strengthen your own bid if you were making one. Grateful for an urgent reply!"

On 16th December I made a one-day fact-finding visit to Uruguay to find out as much as I possibly could about Plan Ceibal and the bid. I tried to see as many people and gather as much information about Plan Ceibal and the project as I possibly could in a single day. I managed to establish that the committee reviewing the bids would consist of six people: Claudia Brovetto and Gabriela Kaplan from Plan Ceibal, Laura Motta from the Ministry of Education, Rosario Estrada from International House and two primary school teachers. I also discovered that six organisations had bought bidding documents, the

Council, Open University and Oxford University Press (though they were not planning to bid), and three others. Pearson was probably the most likely other contender. Rosario Estrada was very helpful and said if we had a chance to bid together with the Open University we should go for it. She thought we would not be able to employ teachers from the private sector in Uruguay as remote teachers and suggested we should train teachers from the state sector (e.g. the Teacher Training College) for this task. The Embassy was also very supportive, offering space for UK and local staff, and agreeing to process a small number of payments each month on our behalf. They also suggested checking whether we still retained our previous status allowing us to employ Uruguayan staff in Uruguay.

We got the green light from the Council in Manchester to go ahead and prepare a bid, and managed to get the deadline for submission extended by just over a month, to the end of January

Meanwhile, Fanta had been to see the doctor because she had blood in her stools. I jokingly said it was probably because she ate far too much hot chilli pepper, but she went to see the doctor just in case. I wrote in mid-January to Kingsway Chapel,

"Please pray for Fanta who has been told she needs a test doing under a general anaesthetic, ideally within the next 2 weeks. She will be on her own most of this time as I am on my way to a meeting in London then working in Manchester next week writing a project bid for Uruguay, due to fly back to Argentina only on 30th January. Otherwise all is well and we have been attending a flourishing Brethren assembly. Though everything is in Spanish, we are getting there slowly with the language.

The Brethren movement turned out to be very well-established in Argentina, with over 1300 congregations throughout the country.

"Brethren work in Argentina is considered to have started with the arrival of John Henry Ewen in 1882, who... inspired and was followed by a number of pioneer missionaries from the UK and other countries. The construction of the railroad network brought many skilled and spiritually gifted individuals who established testimonies in several regions of the country. From 1950 onwards the work mainly transitioned to national leadership. The principles of the autonomy of the local churches, coupled with the fellowship and interrelation among local congregations strengthening the work, effectively continue to this day."[89]

31 January to Lynn Jones at Kingsway Chapel:

"Please continue to pray for Fanta. She is waiting to get the results from a biopsy on a large polyp they have found in her intestine - these should be back on Friday. I don't think it was just a coincidence that yesterday's reading in the *Life Journal* included Exodus 23 verses 25 and 26: - "I will take away sickness from among you. I will give you a full life span".

Then on 2nd February I wrote:

"Unfortunately the biopsy results were not good. The foreign office medical insurers have recommended Fanta should return to the UK for treatment and we are waiting to hear when they have managed to arrange an appointment to see an NHS consultant in Chester. We let out our house so she won't be able to stay there until the beginning of April, so if anyone has a spare room and would like a lodger for a few weeks, do let us know! I have got 5 days compassionate leave and will take a further 5 days off to try and sort something out, but will then have to return to work in Argentina. Please pray for a speedy recovery!"

3rd February to Judith and Norman Goodwin,

"Thank you so much for your kind offer to have Fanta to stay until we can move back into our house. We have arranged to stay for the first few days with my brother Ian and his wife Julie in Hoylake, so it wouldn't be until mid-February, when I'll have to return to work back here in Buenos Aires. I haven't mentioned this possibility to Fanta yet. (She might prefer to stay somewhere close to Arrowe Park hospital if she ends up having to go there more or less every day for treatment.)

We have booked a flight for tomorrow and Fanta has an appointment to see a consultant on Wednesday. It looks as if she will need radiation treatment and possibly surgery. We've given the tenant the necessary two months' notice, so we should be able to move back into our house in Chester from 4th April. I will be back again in March for some meetings in London and a conference in Glasgow. Longer term I guess will depend on how the treatment goes, but it could be quite a long haul!

Yesterday they were on strike at the airport here and blockaded the road - so please pray that our travel arrangements on Saturday go smoothly!

Once we have seen the doctor and have a better idea of what is happening and where, we'll get in touch with you. Thank you so much for your help and support at this difficult time".

5th February to Peter Arnstein:

"We arrived back in Meols this evening after a marathon 27 hour journey from Buenos Aires. The onward flight from Manchester to Heathrow was cancelled because of heavy snow. We would have missed it anyway, because our flight had to wait for ages for a stand to become vacant as no planes were taking off. But we eventually managed to recover our baggage, which had been checked through to Manchester, and got the train from Euston to Liverpool.

Fanta has an appointment for Wednesday morning, after which they are likely to do various tests and then decide on the best course of treatment. But it now increasingly looks as if she faces a pretty tough time over the next three months and maybe longer. I may have to stay here to look after her, which could have implications for my job, Marie's boarding school fees, and so on. Please pray for a speedy recovery for Fanta, peace of mind for both of us, and also for James and Marie.

We know that God is in control, has a plan for our lives and that all things work together for good to those who love Him, who are called according to His purpose".

9th February to Peter Arnstein

"We have found a really nice place to stay from later this month, overlooking the Royal Liverpool golf course, until the tenant vacates our house in Chester. This might be before the end of the lease if she finds somewhere suitable earlier. We are in a bit of a limbo while they do various tests before deciding on the best course of treatment in about three weeks' time. It looks as if I will have to go back to work then, but will be back again a couple of weeks later for some meetings and will stay on for a further week during the Easter holidays. If all goes well after about six months Fanta should be ok to return to Argentina. It's quite a stressful time with possibly quite major decisions looming up and we really appreciate your supporting us in prayer.

To end on a positive note, this has brought us both closer together, and we are already seeing the Lord's hand at work - the flight from Heathrow last Sunday was the last one to land before they closed the airport completely; at any other time of the year it would have been really difficult to find a self-contained suite with kitchen and bathroom in a lovely location where we could stay for a whole six weeks for only £25 a night; and there seems to be a good likelihood of a full recovery, though this might take quite some time."

22 February to Pearl Evans

"Fanta has done various scans and sees the consultant at Arrowe Park on Friday to find out what treatment they are proposing. This will probably be at Clatterbridge Hospital and go on for the next 5-6 weeks. I am hoping to return to Argentina on Monday but will then be back a couple of weeks later and stay in the UK till Easter attending various meetings and also taking some leave. We'll let you know when Fanta will be back in Chester -

in the meantime please keep on praying for a speedy recovery".

28 February to Peter Arnstein

"Please continue to pray for Fanta. She had various scans, and the good news is that the cancer hasn't spread to any other organs. She is about to start a 5-week course of treatment within the next 2-3 weeks.

I had to leave for a meeting in Cuba, where I am at the moment, and after that am going on to Argentina, but will be back in the UK from mid-March to mid-April".

4 March to Fanta

"I have been reading a book about beating cancer by Mark Davies[90] - you should get a copy! The guy who wrote it lives in Chester, had pretty much the same symptoms as you have, and was successfully treated at Clatterbridge hospital by Dr Myint. If you go to the website you can read some of the chapters without buying it, so you can see if you think it's worth reading. I found it really encouraging".

17 March to Peter Arnstein

"Fanta went to the hospital on Thursday and has a treatment plan which starts a week on Monday and goes on for 5 weeks with radiotherapy 5 days a week and chemotherapy tablets as well. She seems to be in good spirits and maintaining a positive attitude.

I arrived back from Argentina on Wednesday morning for two days of meetings in London, then came up to Hoylake last night for the weekend, then I have to go to a conference in Glasgow until Friday. I also have to see a consultant myself a week on Monday about an enlarged prostate (seems quite common in old men but I've had a nasty infection which makes me want to pee all the time, probably exacerbated by stress!)

Please continue to pray for us all! Fanta seems to be in good hands and Clatterbridge has the best oncology centre in the northwest".

On 11th April we were able to move back into our house in Chester following the departure of the tenant, then at the end of the month we had some very good news - Marie phoned up to say she was being made head girl at the Leys School the following year. More good news followed on the Plan Ceibal front:

4 May to Geoff Smith and Michael Carrier

"The proposal with the highest score was the one presented by the British Council. All evaluators gave the British Council the highest score. The British Council had greater experience and the best track record in projects linked to the objectives of the Plan Ceibal English language programme. The BC proposal was clearly connected to curricular content at an adequate academic level for this age group. The lesson plans took into account the diversity of groups, the language level of the classroom teacher, were easy to follow for the teacher through the translation into Spanish and the curricular design included the four skills. In the BC proposal the work of the classroom and remote teachers were clearly integrated in the classroom. BC showed a clear predisposition to working with the client to develop the project and highlighted the collaborative nature of the work between the classroom teacher and the remote teacher".

So to all intents and purposes we had won the bid! But everything was by no means yet done and dusted. Some further clarification from Plan Ceibal followed.

"The realization of the "proof of concept" by the British Council is approved during 2012 (July - November), that will be considered as an additional stage of the evaluation, prior to the final award of the entire project. This additional stage will be held at the 20 selected schools for the pilot project."

5th May to Lynn Jones

"Some things to thank God for and to pray about from the Woods family - Marie has just heard she is going to be Head Girl at the Leys School next year. We are very proud of her! Fanta' s treatment was stopped for a couple of weeks but should be over before the end of May. It seems to be working and she's no longer having to take painkillers. I've just heard the British Council has won a 5-month contract to do the pilot phase for a much bigger project to teach English remotely in Uruguay, for which I'll be the Programme Manager. Thanks be to God!"

By this stage the details of how exactly we were going to handle the proof of concept stage had been agreed with Plan Ceibal. However, getting the video-conferencing technology to work was not always straightforward. On 10th May I wrote to colleagues in Argentina and the UK,

"All attempts to connect 3 ways (UK, Argentina and dialling out to Uruguay) ended in failure, as the call either couldn't be connected by dialling out or dropped when connected by the operator. Let's hope we have more success with videoconferencing for remote teaching! In the end I just talked with Claudia and Gabriella myself, without Mary taking part from Argentina.

By mid-May we had agreed with Claudia and Gabriella that there would be two five-day orientation courses, the first from 4-9 June for 10 teachers from 5 schools. Trainers were still to be identified but could include Andrei Tarassov from Colombia (either face to face or remotely via videoconferencing), Sylvia Retarroli, Cristina Banfi, Gabriella Madera and a UK trainer. The content would cover

(1) The syllabus

(2) Lessons to be taught, for as many weeks as are available by the start of the course

(3) Methodology – practising/using language. How to support the remote teacher

(4) Language improvement – starting an appropriate online course such as Learn English Pathways Elementary under supervision

(5) Teachers would take a simple test to establish their language level in advance of being assigned to the appropriate on-line course.

A similar course would be given from June 25 – 29 for two parallel groups of 20 Classroom Teachers. Trainers would repeat the content for each group. There would be 20 schools in the pilot. Some of these had two schools (shifts). So altogether there would be 50 groups, each with 1 class teacher. Four of the selected schools had a specialist English teacher and pupils might already know some English. In these schools the remote teaching would need to fit with the Specialist teacher's timetable, and the

Remote Teachers would need to handle their involvement carefully as they would be able to do a lot more on their own. The Specialist teachers were all located in the north. The school day in most schools ran from 0800 to 1200, but in some schools there was a second shift from 1300 to 1700.

Ideally the children would be tested as soon as possible, before the materials were written. The expectation was that most pupils would have virtually no knowledge of English. Plan Ceibal were not expecting a rigorous evaluation of progress in English in the Proof of Concept phase. Testing could however take place in the 3rd or 4th week of the course.

Remote Teaching would start in 5 schools (10 groups) on 11 June, and in the other 20 or so schools (40 groups) on 23 July. English classes would end at the end of November.

For Language Improvement for the teachers, we would start with the pilot schools group of 50 classroom teachers, with a ratio of one e-moderator to 15-25 class teachers, then extend this to a further 50 teachers (self-selected) in October.

We were waiting for confirmation from BC Global Solutions in Manchester on who would lead on sorting out the video-conferencing facilities in Colombia, Argentina and Mexico to ensure they were technically of an adequate standard and liaise via Claudia with the Plan Ceibal Technical team

We would recruit a full time Project Manager on a 6 months renewable contract to be based in Uruguay.

Materials, as well as being quality reviewed by a BC person (to be identified) would be reviewed by the Plan

Ceibal team and would be available in soft and hard copy. Plan Ceibal could distribute hard copies within 2-3 days. They were also willing to print smallish quantities of materials on our behalf in the early stages of the Proof of Concept before we got our own project staff in place in Uruguay.

One of the songs they sang regularly at the Iglesia Cristiana Evangelica in Buenos Aires which was a great encouragement to me at this time was *Rompiendo en Fe*:

> Every time my faith is tested
> You give me the grace to grow a little more.
> The mountains and valleys, deserts and seas which I cross bring me closer to you.
> My trials are not greater than my God
> And they will not prevent me from going forward.
> If the sea opens in front of me,
> God can make me walk on the waters.
> Overcoming by faith, my life will be clothed with your power.
> Overcoming by faith, with boldness I will see the supernatural.
> Sowing and growing, I will fight and overcome,
> Living every day overcoming by faith.

Just as my entire leave allocation for the year was about to run out and the British Council was suggesting one possible option could be to take unpaid leave if I wanted to remain in the UK any longer, I had been smitten with an incredibly painful urinary infection which made me want to pee urgently every half hour or so. Driving down the motorway was a complete nightmare.

Whether this was a case of mind over matter, a result of acute stress, or some form of divine intervention, I will never know. But it meant that the GP signed me off work initially for three weeks, then once I had recovered I still had to do various tests over the course of the next three weeks. So I managed to get signed off on sick leave for six weeks altogether, which enabled me to stay alongside Fanta and support her at a time when her treatment was really starting to take its toll. Towards the end of May I returned to Argentina.

21 May to Fanta

"Tried to call you on your mobile but it keeps cutting off and nobody is answering the house phone either! Ian said you saw Dr Myint who said the tumour had 80 per cent disappeared and might disappear completely over the next few weeks. Let's keep on praying that it does! It's horrible weather here - dull wet and windy. Ian said it was nice and sunny in Chester, so maybe you are in the best place. I will try to call you tonight on Skype. I arrived ok and my luggage also".

31st May to Peter

"Fanta has come to the end of her radio and chemo-therapy, but it's a bit like microwaving stuff, the effects continue after the oven is switched off! She is suffering quite a lot in the hot weather and her skin is really sensitive to going out in the sun. But the good news is that the last scan she had showed that the treatment had reduced the tumour by about 80 % and the consultant was amazed at the results. Now she has to wait and see for the next ten weeks when they will decide if she needs an operation.

I had to return to Argentina last week to get the project the British Council has won in Uruguay off the ground. But the good thing about Skype is we probably talk more from a distance than when we were living in the same house!

Please do carry on praying for a full recovery for Fanta. I think both of us have realized the truth of the hymn which goes "Only one life, 'twill soon be past, Only what's done for Christ will last." We need to make the most of our lives while we can, and focus on the things that really matter!"

I wrote a speech in Spanish for the opening ceremony of the first orientation course for classroom teachers:

"Last Sunday on the subte in Buenos Aires I noticed an advert for maths courses which quoted the founder, a Japanese named Kumon. He said, 'La ensenanza individual sera el corriente mas importante del siglo veinte e uno' (Individual learning will be the most important trend of the 21st century). I thought to myself, that is very true, and indeed the Ceibal English Project is an excellent example of individual learning. As we all know, Uruguay was the first country in the world to give every student in government schools a laptop. This means that students are no longer dependent on the teacher or a small number of textbooks but potentially they have access to a huge variety of resources on the internet. It also means the role of the teacher changes, at least to some extent. She or he is no longer the main source of information for students, but more of a facilitator and guide who is learning alongside the students themselves. I think it's important we all understand this. We are about to embark on a very ambitious project, which, if it succeeds, will revolutionise the way English is taught, not only in Uruguay, but in many other countries around the world. We are beginning in a very small way, with a proof of concept for the project, starting in June in just 10 classes, then from the beginning of August extending the project to a further 40 classes. We do not yet have all the answers, although we do have many questions! As far as I am aware, nowhere else in the world has anyone tried to teach a language to large classes of primary school pupils using tele-presence technology. There have been projects in the UK to teach English and Latin to small numbers of online students, and a few years ago the British Council ran a project using teachers in Germany to teach a small class of adult students in Serbia. You may have seen some controversial adverts for English courses online where Argentinian and Costa Rican teachers are compared unfavourably with blonde American native speaker teachers offering one to one English courses for adults. But this will be the first time English has been taught to such young pupils in such large numbers. I understand most of you have not studied English before, but you shouldn't let this worry you! As well as preparing you thoroughly for the practice lessons each week which you will be organising to follow up on the remote lessons, we intend to provide you with an online course of English language improvement at your own current level. On Saturday you will be meeting Gabriela Madera, who will be acting as a trainer and mentor for the online language improvement course, which is called Learn English

Pathways. Each level of this course takes about 35 hours to complete, and by following this course at your own pace and in your own time, you will be building up your confidence to teach the practice lessons. It can be done! I have only been learning Spanish for a year, since a few months before I arrived in Argentina last October. To start with, I worked my way quickly through all the beginners levels of the Instituto Cervantes' online Spanish course, then took the placement test for a face to face course and was put in at the intermediate level. I then found I had to unlearn quite a lot of what I had taught myself , because the online course was good for grammar, vocabulary, reading and listening, but not so good for teaching speaking! A lot will depend on staying motivated, and Gabriela will be holding regular teleconferences and replying to emails and postings on Moodle to answer your questions and clear up any doubts you may have. In the short term, we are going to be very dependent on remote teachers, but in the longer term, the project will only be sustainable and affordable if we can create a cadre of Uruguayan teachers of English within the state system who are able to teach English just as well as they currently teach all the other subjects on the primary school curriculum.

We are hoping to recruit a Uruguayan Project Manager, to be based in Montevideo, who will be responsible for the smooth running of the project on a day to day basis. This will facilitate communication with you and the Plan Ceibal team and avoid the problems of managing the project from a distance. 50 years ago, the British Council had an office in Montevideo. We are not planning to reopen an office here, but the fact that we are managing the Ceibal English project should definitely strengthen ties between our two countries. It's not much more than a month since we heard that Plan Ceibal was giving us the contract for the proof of concept phase of the project. This is not a long time to write materials, plan an orientation course, translate tests, set up an online platform and make sure the technology works. So I expect there will be some hitches / problems and ask you to be patient. We are all breaking new ground together here, and the contribution, commitment and enthusiasm of every single one of you will be vital to the success of the project".

14 August 2012 to Lynn Jones

"Please pray for Fanta who is having an operation to remove a bowel tumour tomorrow at Arrowe Park hospital. I am flying back from Argentina tonight but she will have had to set off for the hospital before I arrive there.

She is likely to be in hospital for a week afterwards and then will probably have to carry on with more chemotherapy for the next six months.

It's quite a stressful time as our family is all now in different places! James starts year 2 of his Games Design course in Birmingham in September, Marie will be doing her last year at boarding school in Cambridge with the added responsibility of being head girl. The project I'm managing in Uruguay to teach English remotely is going well - in fact I'm going to miss the official launch by the President of Uruguay on Wednesday.

If all goes according to plan, I'll be going returning to Argentina on 5th September. If however there are any complications I may have to arrange to stay and work in Manchester for a few weeks".

From Maria Isabel Arn
"Dear Paul,

I hope you and your wife are fine. I just wanted to ask you about her health. I am part of a Catholic prayer group: we are praying for you and your family.
Kind regards.
Maria Isabel
Plan Ceibal Project Officer".

What I did not mention to people was that this day was probably the worst day of my life. I went straight to the hospital from the airport and arrived just in time to see Fanta before she was taken off to the pre-op ward. She was scheduled to have the operation in mid-morning and they told me she should be back on the ward by around 3 p.m. It was a beautiful sunny day and I went for a walk in the fields at the back of the hospital, all the time praying hard that God would guide the surgeon and watch over Fanta. By 2.00 p.m. there was no sign of her coming out of the operating theatre, so I adjourned to a nearby pub for a beer and a burger, although I didn't have much of an appetite. By 3.00 p.m. I went back to enquire on progress, but they said she was still in the operating theatre. By now I was starting to get a bit anxious, and at 4.00 p.m. it was the same story. When I inquired again at 5.00 o'clock, only to be told she still hadn't returned from the operating theatre, I was starting to get desperate. The nurse tried to reassure me that sometimes these operations took a long time. Finally at 6.30 there was a call from the surgeon to say that she was now in the recovery room and would be back on the ward within the next half hour or so. It subsequently came to light that she was allergic to the anaesthetics used and suffered bronchospasm when she was anaesthetised. The hospital later sent her for an appointment at Broadgreen Hospital the following March to avoid any potentially fatal complications with anaesthesia the next time she had to have an operation.

That evening I wrote to Lynn Jones:

"Fanta has had her operation and is now recovering. She will be in Ward 17 at Arrowe Park hospital for about a week. Please pray that she will avoid any complications and get back on her feet again quickly!"

Shortly prior to this we had taken on Dario Banegas as the Plan Ceibal Project Manager, based in Buenos Aires. Dario described the proof of concept phase of the project in some detail in a scholarly article published in Innovation in Language Learning and Teaching.[91]

Both Dario and I had to make frequent trips to Montevideo, generally staying for two or three days, several times a month. I became quite adept at taking advantage of my diplomatic status to take 50 inch tv screens which were half the price in Argentina compared to Uruguay across with me each time on the ferry. Altogether I must have taken around twelve of these with me on different visits. On one of these visits I was staying in a hotel near the airport called Hosteria del Lago, which was built on sloping ground next to a lake. On checking in, I had noticed that there was a six-inch step where the level of the bedroom floor changed half way across the room. Waking up in the middle of the night to use the bathroom, I didn't bother switching the light on and crashed into the step with my big toe, breaking the nail. This eventually fell out and another nail grew, but for several months afterwards I was in considerable pain.

Around this time I wrote to James Shipton, the Director in Argentina, saying, "If this project is going to work in the longer term, we will need a project manager based in Uruguay from January 2013 onwards. We (or Plan Ceibal) will also need to employ Uruguayan remote teachers as well as teachers from other countries. They have already bowed to pressure and now agree, despite some reservations, that the latter is a sensible course of action".

At the end of August I wrote to Ann Thorogood:

"Many thanks for your prayers and good wishes. Please continue to remember us in prayer - although Fanta is recovering satisfactorily from the operation, she is in considerable pain, and the effects of her medication is really taking its toll on her. I am just hoping that things begin to return to normal fairly soon".

A few weeks later I wrote to the British Council

"I am just coming to the end of three weeks annual/ mid-tour leave which I took to coincide with my wife having an operation (ileostomy). If all goes well she will need another operation in about 6-8 weeks' time to reverse this. After that she will need further chemotherapy, but will probably be allowed to return to Argentina. She seems to be getting over the operation reasonably well, although there is a part of the scar which has still not closed up properly.

I asked the nurse if it would be necessary to return to the UK to coincide with when she has the next operation, and she advised that it would probably be inadvisable for her to be left on her own for a couple of weeks afterwards, as she might not be able to lift things.

However, I have used up all my annual leave for this year. Would it possible to arrange to work again in Manchester for 2 - 3 weeks if necessary, as I did last April, subject to my line manager's agreement? It's a bit hard to plan for, as the dates may only be decided at quite short notice.

And is it possible to claim the airfare for this as a compassionate journey? Alternatively, because my children are entitled to child holiday visits which neither of them has used since last December, could I claim for a reverse child holiday visit ticket and thus kill two birds with one stone?"

The Human Resources team were actually very helpful and readily agreed that I could work in Manchester for several weeks as well as claiming for a compassionate journey.

By the third week in September I was back in Argentina, attending the FAAPI Conference in San Martin de los Andes. It was snowing heavily when we arrived and the snow-covered peaks were quite spectacular.

I submitted an article for the English and Exams newsletter:

"The Uruguayans are so pleased with our remote teaching of English pilot that they now want us to start negotiating on a national scheme which will require an astonishing 1,000 hours a week of remote teacher time from January", says Regional Council Director for the Americas Christopher Wade. The formal launch of the project, by Minister of Education Ricardo Ehrlich, accompanied by the CEO of Plan Ceibal, Miguel Brechner and Director Argentina James Shipton, took place on 15th August 2012 at School Number 6, in Pan de Azucar. There was excellent coverage in the local press, on TV, and on the Ministry of Education website. "Ceibal en Ingles" is a program for children and teachers at primary school level, which offers the opportunity for pupils to learn English via tele-presence technology, whilst at the same time developing classroom teachers' English proficiency. Remote lessons are delivered via a weekly one hour videoconference where the remote teacher interacts with children and class teachers in real time. This year we are teaching classes from the British Council Teaching Centre in Colombia and from the Cultura Inglesa (AACI) in Argentina. Next year the intention is to incorporate remote Uruguayan teachers also. The local classroom teachers, who usually have only a very limited knowledge of English, are taking the online Learn English Pathways course, supported by mentors who monitor their progress and provide encourage and support. The children have access to Learn English materials on their OLPC laptops. These materials are being transferred to CREA, a new content management platform hosted by Plan Ceibal. Currently the program is being implemented in 50 classes from 20 different schools. All the local teachers involved were invited to join voluntarily, driven by their motivation to learn English. They receive training and mentoring support from the remote teachers to plan and then deliver two follow-up lessons each week where the language presented in the remote lesson is practised extensively and used in communicative contexts."

By the end of September we had agreed that the project would aim to increase the number of remote lessons to 1050 lessons per week in 2013 (200 schools), 3000 lessons per week in 2014 (400 schools) and up to 5000 lessons per week in 2015. There was some discussion about staging the expansion during 2013 so that 500 classes per week would be taught from March and 1000 per week from August.

The arguments in favour of staged expansion were based on quality considerations, the availability of suitable trainers, the absorptive capacity of the system, cost, and lack of clarity on locations of all class teachers until their postings for the year had been finalised by mid-February. The technical capability was to be installed in 250 schools by March, and video-conferencing equipment installed or upgraded in Argentina at the Cultura Inglesa and in Colombia at the British Council.

Plan Ceibal agreed they would recruit and pay for remote teachers within Uruguay from key private language schools. They were keen for us to set up a British Council project office in Montevideo. One possibility would be to relocate Dario's Project Manager post to Montevideo from early 2013, and possibly to move my post to Montevideo. This would require the agreement of senior British Council management and the UK-based post could fall under the umbrella of the existing Anglo-Uruguayan technical cooperation agreement, a copy of which had been unearthed by the Embassy. Meanwhile

Dario would have use of a desk at Plan Ceibal. We also explored the idea of recruiting ten low-cost "Language Assistants" from the UK for March 2013 and 30 for August 2013, with an allowance of US $500 per month each. There would be other associated costs including orientation courses, management costs in UK and Argentina, and they could be attached to language schools, possibly dispersed across the country. Based on our initial estimates, the teaching cost per class hour per pupil would be US$ 1.5 approx. We also began to look into the possibility of setting up a virtual teaching centre in the Philippines or Eastern Europe, but considered this would be unlikely to be fully operational for at least 12 months, if at all. Provided the costs were affordable it could however be a source of high quality remote teaching from 2014 onwards.

Fanta's ordeal was not yet over. On 8 October I wrote to the FCO Healthline:

"I understand that Fanta is about to start a further six-month course of chemotherapy with injections every two weeks, then only after that they will do an operation to reverse the ilieostomy. She is going to see the doctor next Thursday about starting the chemotherapy".

I had hoped she would be able to come to Argentina for a couple of weeks at Christmas, along with our two children, but according to my GP brother she was likely to get very prone to infections and it would not be advisable for her to travel (the journey door to door took about 20 hours). So I made plans to return to the UK for some leave at Christmas.

In October I wrote to Malu Vilches, a Filipino ELT expert I had known in Manila, enquiring about the possibility of using Filipinos for remote teaching. This would be one way of keeping costs down, whilst at the same time providing high quality teaching.

"You probably won't remember me - I used to be the British Council Assistant Representative in Manila from 1987 to 1991. I'm currently managing a pilot project to teach English remotely to children in primary schools in Uruguay via video-conferencing. By 2015 they want us to scale up to deliver 5000 remote lessons a week. I have read that a lot of Koreans are being taught remotely from The Philippines and wonder if you can put me in touch with any reputable organisations that might be able to deliver remote lessons with good quality teaching at an affordable price, or that might be interested in setting up a "virtual teaching centre" based in The Philippines".

The British Council in London was quite sceptical about both Language Assistants and Filipino teachers. Esther Hay wrote,

"With the time it is taking to engage with the Philippines, it may be better to concentrate on sources in the Americas for the next phase, and look at further expansion later. It would be best to source in countries where we already have British Council representation, and look for qualified/experienced teachers through the Council where we have an office (and Teaching Centre) from the Latin American Culturas, or similar organisations, (rather than Language Assistants) to ensure quality delivery and reduce risk".

In December I wrote to Michael Carrier in London:

"A bit of gossip - the Uruguayan institutions seem to have formed a cartel and demanded $50 per hour for remote teaching, but Ceibal beat them down to $25. They are not happy as they won't make any profit, but this means that our own offer to provide Filipino teachers at $20 per 45 minute lesson doesn't look too far out of line. It looks like I will have to move to Uruguay, though apparently that will increase costs to the Council. In Argentina I currently enjoy diplomatic status, but there is no double taxation agreement between the UK and Uruguay, so if I'm classed as resident in Uruguay they would have to pay 35% tax on my salary and allowances. I am not exactly overjoyed, having moved twice in the past two years already, but I guess moving to Uruguay will have its compensations (nice beaches, less crime, more relaxed lifestyle...)".

On 18 December I wrote to Fred Heath:

"I will be moving across the river to Montevideo as the Plan Ceibal Programme Manager in April if all goes well and we get a deal signed in the next couple of weeks. I would then retire in late 2014, having set everything up and handed over to a local Project Manager to see things through to completion.

Unfortunately last February Fanta had to return to the UK to be treated under the NHS. She had an operation in September and is now on six months chemotherapy. This week she developed deep vein thrombosis but they have now got her on blood thinning drugs as well as the chemo, so hopefully she will get over it quickly. At present her leg is hot, swollen and painful, but better today than it was yesterday. By next May she should be fully recovered and they expect to have eradicated all traces of the cancer.

James dropped out of Biology at Leeds and is now doing Computer Games Design in Birmingham. He seems to be enjoying the course though spends an awful lot of time playing games, not just designing them! Marie is doing well - she is now in her final year at boarding school in Cambridge. She wants to do English Lit at university and now has offers from four out of the five universities she applied to. One is still to come (from Durham), which said they were not making any offers till the new year. She is contemplating re-applying next year to Oxford if she manages to get all As and A *s at A level".

Early in the new year I wrote to Richard Webber, my former Line Manager in Manchester:

"I spent the afternoon rewriting my c.v. as I got approached a few days ago by a headhunting agency who are recruiting a Director Africa for the Centre for British Teachers. Don't think I stand much chance, but it's worth having a go.

Fanta is half way through 6 months of chemo. It's taking its toll - the day I arrived back for Christmas she had to rush off to hospital and was found to have a blood clot in her leg - a side effect of the chemotherapy. Also her white blood cell count is now very low, leaving her prone to infections - so she is avoiding crowded places like the cinema and shops as far as possible. But she is a very strong character and if anyone can defeat it, she will.

If I don't get the CFBT job I'm probably going to have to move to Montevideo in April as Programme Manager for the Plan Ceibal Project. We are hopefully about to sign a three-year contract next week, but the Council's Executive Board has to approve opening a branch of the British Council in Uruguay first. I suggested they could make me the Country Director, but they want to have their cake and eat it by getting me to spend 50% of my time on the Plan Ceibal Project and 50% on doing the things which a Country Director would do, but without the title, kudos or any extra pay.

British Council doesn't change its spots....."

The plans were approved at Board level and I began to set things in motion for moving across the River Plate from Buenos Aires to Montevideo.

Dario and his partner were not at all keen on moving to Montevideo, and after some agonising he decided not to extend his contract for a further period. We were able to recruit Graham Stanley to replace him as Project Manager. Graham had extensive experience and contacts in Computer Assisted Language Learning and related fields, was fluent in Spanish, and we set things in motion for him to fly out to Uruguay within the next few weeks.

The bureaucracy involved in transferring to Montevideo seemed at times to be insurmountable. In order to apply for residency in Uruguay you had to get a document from everywhere you had lived in the previous five years. In my case this included Botswana. I wrote to a contact in the British Embassy:

"I am currently working for the British Council in Argentina and managing a large-scale project in Uruguay. The British Council has now had FCO and Board of Trustees approval to set up a branch in Uruguay, where we are not currently represented. I would then become the legal representative of the British Council in Uruguay.

In order to get the residency process moving in Uruguay, I need a certificate from the police in every country where I have lived for the past 5 years confirming that I have a clean criminal record. The process for

Argentina seems to be relatively straightforward (it only took two days!) and I expect to be able to download the document today.

Botswana, however is proving problematic. The High Commission in Botswana (Nomsa) has confirmed they will assist with obtaining the necessary document from the Botswana Police Dept, but they need a set of fingerprints to be sent from here. I was advised by the local Comisario to go to the Dir. Informacion de Antecedentes on the third floor of Azopardo 670, where after some considerable hesitation they took several sets of prints manually and said these would be processed by Friday. They could not just give me them to take away and post myself to Botswana. They would not accept a letter from the British Council signed by James Shipton but said they needed something "official". Can you help?"

Armed with a letter from the High Commission, I returned on the Friday to collect the fingerprints, but there was someone else there who insisted "These fingerprints are ours" and refused to hand them over. After a lengthy argument I gave up.

The last resort was to approach Interpol. They appeared to have an office in Palermo, not far from the Museum of Modern Art. On rolling up at the reception desk and explaining that I needed my fingerprints taking, I was wheeled in promptly to the office of the Director, who sent for someone with an ink pad and very obligingly produced a set of fingerprints there and then, explaining to me that his staff really needed English lessons and could the British Council help?

3rd May to Geoff Thompson

"Thank you and the folks at Kingsway for your prayers and support for Fanta. She saw the surgeon today at Arrowe Park and they are scheduling an operation for mid-June to restore everything back to normal. I think she will be greatly relieved to get rid of the colostomy bag!

I finally got the green light to sign the lease on a flat in Montevideo after a lot of frustrating delays because we still hadn't signed the main contract with Plan Ceibal.

If all goes well, I should be moving from Argentina to Uruguay within the next 2 weeks. The flat I'm hoping to rent is about five minutes' walk from the office and nearest shopping centre, ten minutes from the church (the building is shared between an English-speaking international church and a Spanish-speaking Baptist church) and ten minutes' walk from the beach - which looks quite remarkably like the promenade at Hoylake! There are still quite a few headaches ahead including sorting out a sub-contract with a supplier in The Philippines to deliver up to 2000 remote English lessons each week by next March, and if all goes well increasing this to 4800 lessons a week the following year.

I hope to be back in Chester for three weeks in June, coinciding with Fanta's operation."

Later in May I made a flying visit to the Philippines to tie up the arrangements for remote teaching with "Smile Means English" (SME) in Cebu. I e-mailed Fanta:

"I arrived safely here in Manila after a marathon flight via Dubai - I left at 6 p.m. on Thursday evening and arrived here at the hotel at 6 p.m. on Saturday evening. Feeling distinctly jet-lagged, so am going to force myself to stay awake a bit longer, then take a Melatonin tablet and hope to sleep for 8 hours solidly, then wake up on

Filipino time!

The hotel they booked for me is near the junction of EDSA and Ortigas, literally two minutes' walk from Greenhills Christian Fellowship which we used to go to when we lived here, so I don't have any excuse for not going to church tomorrow morning!"

After meetings with the British Council Director, who appeared completely disinterested in the Ceibal project and was anyway due to retire a few months later, as well as meetings with various other Council staff, I flew on that evening to Cebu, had various meetings with the SME Director and staff, inspected their existing remote teaching facilities and the proposed premises for the new remote teaching centre, tested out the videoconferencing link with Montevideo and left feeling reassured that, provided we strictly controlled the quality of the teaching staff they recruited, they would be able to deliver.

10 URUGUAY

At the beginning of July 2013 I moved to Uruguay, taking several suitcases with me on the three hour ferry journey, and spending the first couple of nights in a completely empty flat with only an airbed (which collapsed slowly during the night) and a cooker. I had despatched our heavy baggage a few days earlier using a firm named Crown Relocations. Although it was only a short trip by ferry across the river, this was the last we would see of our baggage for the next nine months. I started getting impatient after six months or so when the agent they had nominated at the Uruguay end kept saying he had heard absolutely nothing from Crown Relocations in Argentina. Finally in desperation I wrote to their London office and they eventually replied saying they had closed down their office in Argentina several months earlier. A few weeks later the crates finally turned up in Montevideo. Hiring a van and driving over on the ferry myself might have been quicker and easier!

In July there was an email from a friend in Botswana who was about to move to Costa Rica and needed a police clearance certificate, asking how I went about getting mine. I replied,

"It took forever! After unsuccessful attempts to persuade the Argentine police to let me have a set of fingerprints (they were quite happy to take them but then refused to hand them over) I ended up going to Interpol who let me have a set. I then sent them to the British Embassy in Botswana who extracted a police report from the Botswana police. This then had to be sent to the nearest Uruguayan consulate - in South Africa - which refused to take anything other than cash payments, (so a runner had to take the money in cash from Botswana). The document was then "apostilled" (notarised). It subsequently arrived back in Buenos Aires with a note to the effect that the apostille was valid everywhere apart from Uruguay! Good luck! I would contact your embassy in Gaborone and ask them to assist.

I emailed Fanta, James and Marie to let them know I was now in Uruguay:

"Got here ok. Have signed up for a phone and internet to be installed on 8 July. Till then I should be able to call you on Skype from the office around 5 p.m. here which is 9 p.m. in UK. Tomorrow am going to look for a fridge, bed, washing machine, sofa, table and chairs...the airbed seems to leak a bit!"

Then two days later:

"The lady who was going to take me to look for furniture didn't turn up, because she was trying to get the lights turned back on for our new project manager, whose electricity had been cut off!"

And on 6th July:

"Trying out the new washing machine. Fridge and microwave work well but the cheap Chinese clothes hanger/drier I bought fell apart even before I reached the flat. Furniture is very expensive here. Have bought a bed, sofa, table, dining chairs and two Ikea-style chairs with wooden arms. Total 3900 dollars...but persuaded the Regional Director that the amount they had given me for buying furniture wasn't enough.

Tomorrow I'm going to check out Christchurch in Carrasco for the first time on a Sunday. It has services in English as well as Spanish. Now I'm worried the sofa I bought won't fit, either to go up the narrow stairs or in the lift. You can saw sofas in half to take them out, but not to get them in!" The delivery men managed to lower it down using ropes from the roof and get it into the flat through the patio doors on the balcony.

I had agreed to give some talks at the LABCI Conference in Peru and had arranged for 600 copies of an article I wrote for EL Gazette to be sent from the UK to the hotel where I would be staying. Fortunately these arrived in Lima by the second day of the three-day conference.

Even brand new flats in Uruguay had a fireplace and chimney for a wood log fire in the living room, and during the Uruguayan winter it got quite cold at night. I wrote to Marie, "The wood fire is ok most of the time but at one point last night while I was in the kitchen with the extractor fan turned on, it sucked all the air back down the chimney and filled the entire flat with dense black smoke."

By April 2014 Fanta was fully recovered and had been

signed off as fit and well enough to return to Uruguay. There was an amusing but scary incident when I was flying back from an ELT conference in Panama soon after she arrived. I had to change planes in Bogota and because there was an earlier flight than the one which I was booked on, I arrived back in Montevideo at 1.30 a.m. rather than at noon the following day. I took a taxi to the flat, climbed the stairs and tried to unlock the front door. However, the key would not turn to open the door, presumably because Fanta had gone to bed leaving the key in the lock. I then banged loudly on the door a few times, but there was no response. Thinking she must have closed all the doors between the front door and the bedroom, I banged again a few times, but to no avail. So I thought the best thing to do was to phone her. Her phone rang several times but there was no answer. I thought either she must be sleeping really soundly or maybe she had been taken ill and was unconscious inside the flat. I tried ringing Marie, James and my brother Ian in the UK, but they hadn't heard anything from her. I banged on the door a few more times, before deciding there wasn't much else I could do at 2.00 a.m. and the best thing was probably to go downstairs to the entrance hall where there was a small sofa on which I could curl up and try to get some sleep. Winter was approaching in Uruguay and it was distinctly chilly in the draughty hallway. After about half an hour, I thought to myself, maybe if I get a long pole, go up on the roof and bang on the bedroom window, if she's there, that might wake her up. So I got the pole used for cleaning the swimming pool, went up on the roof, leaned over the edge of the balcony and tapped for a couple of minutes on the bedroom window below.

Still no response! I put on all the warm clothes I had with me, lay down on the sofa and slept fitfully for several hours. Around 6.00 a.m. I decided to have yet another go at knocking on the door of the flat, and shouted "Fanta, are you there, open the door!" After a minute or so, I heard the key turning in the lock and there was Fanta! It turned out that she had heard me knocking the first time and because she wasn't expecting me back till lunchtime the next day had jumped to the conclusion that thieves must be trying to break in. When the knocking carried on, she was even more convinced it must be thieves and had hidden in an empty trunk in the spare bedroom and closed the lid. Then when she heard knocking on the window she was terrified out of her wits and assumed the thieves were trying to break the window and enter the flat that way. She had spent the rest of the night hunched up inside the trunk imagining the thieves were going to burst in at any moment. When I asked her why she hadn't answered the phone, she said she had assumed the thieves had somehow got hold of her number, so she had ignored it. Why hadn't I shouted to her that it was me? I protested that I hadn't thought on to shout out, as I'd assumed she would hear me knocking. We had a good laugh about this incident afterwards, but Marie said we needed to get much better at communicating with each other.

Carnival in Uruguay was less spectacular than in Brazil, but went on for an extended period of around a month, starting in early February, when the poor neighbourhoods of Sur and Palermo in Montevideo organise the so-called *Desfile de Llamadas,* with loud drumming which can be heard from several blocks away.

Candombe was the rhythm that not only joined the descendants of former slaves together but also reminded them of their African past and their origins and history.

Several places stand out in my memories of Uruguay. The former meat processing plant in the small coastal town of Frey Bentos is now a Unesco World Heritage site. According to the Observer, "Many people who recognise the name are astonished to find out that it is really a town, as opposed to the British brand of canned meat products, originally corned beef and then ready-made pies. It's actually both. The sleepy, charming riverside town in Uruguay, was also home to the Fray Bentos brand which began in 1863 in a sprawling factory. In its heyday this cathedral of the industrial age, built along the town's lush riverbank, fed half the world, churning out corned and frozen beef to fuel wars and the rise of empires. It played such a role in the transformation of how we eat worldwide, bringing meals into the industrial era, that three years ago Unesco declared the abandoned and ruined complex a world heritage site."[92] The plant was founded by Leibig, a German inventor whose "meat extract" a liquid precursor to Oxo, needed vast quantities of beef, so he came to Uruguay where cows were plentiful and cheap. Even today Uruguay has a population of 2 million people but 10 million cows! At its height the plant was processing up to 7000 cows per day, and the meat was either canned as corned beef, or frozen and kept in an enormous seven-storey cold store before being exported all over the world. Meat from Fray Bentos fed troops in both world wars, and British troops even nicknamed one tank Fray Bentos, a dark joke about a crew that were little more than minced meat in a can. A small museum tells the plant's history and features curiosities such as a pickled two-headed calf and Uruguay's first light bulb.

Cabo Polonia is a protected area of great natural beauty which can only be accessed by safari truck from the park gate, or by foot or horseback along the beach from a nearby town called Valizas. There is a village of tiny ranches and huts near the beach, with a lighthouse on an exposed promontory. Next to the lighthouse, you can watch huge colonies of sea lions sunbathing on the rocks. I stayed in a beautiful little guest house overlooking the beach where you could sit in a hammock sipping your cocktail while admiring the view.

Colonia de Sacramento, another Unesco world heritage site is easily accessible on a fast ferry from Buenos Aires and is one of the oldest settlements in Uruguay, dating back to the 1680s. It frequently changed hands between the Spanish and Portuguese. Some of the attractions within easy walking distance of the main square (Plaza Mayor) include the City Gate with its wooden drawbridge, the lighthouse from which you get an excellent view over the town, the Basilica of the Holy Sacrament, built of stone by the Portuguese in 1808, and seven museums all of which are accessible with a single entrance ticket. When we went there with the Hash House Harriers for the weekend we stayed in a cheap hostel which turned out to be swarming with fleas!

One of the places I found quite fascinating was the former Miguelete prison, part of which has now been turned into a contemporary art gallery. Miguelete, which housed inmates from 1888 until 1986 is the oldest panoptic prison - a facility built so that all its parts can be monitored from one central point - preserved in Latin

America in its original condition. Similar buildings in Buenos Aires and Lima were demolished,

Not long before I left Uruguay, the Regional Director, Christopher Wade, who was based in Miami, accompanied Mark Robson, the British Council's Global Director for English from London, on a brief visit to Uruguay. We treated them to 5-star luxury at the Sofitel Hotel Carrasco, where Paul McCartney had stayed a few weeks earlier, took them to see Miguel Brechner at Plan Ceibal, arranged a visit to a rural secondary school where they could see remote teaching by video-conferencing in action and generally wined and dined them. They appeared to be suitably impressed.

After thirty-eight years' service I was hoping I might retire from the Council at the end of the year with some significant token of recognition like an engraved watch or pewter tankard, but what I actually got was a letter signed by the CEO, Martin Davidson, and a straw hat from Christopher Wade.

Shortly before Christmas 2014 there was a wild round of leaving parties, lunches and dinners. Then at 6.00 a.m. on 14th December, en route back to Manchester, I had a couple of glasses of champagne courtesy of Air France somewhere over the Azores to celebrate the end of my life as a cultural diplomat and the beginning of life after the British Council.

11 BIBLIOGRAPHY

1   Phillipson, R, 1992, Linguistic Imperialism

2   Leonard, 'Diplomacy by Other Means' quoted in
     https://www.demos.co.uk/files/Cultural_diplomacy_-_web.pdf
     retrieved on 10.1.2019

3   Cruz, I, Filipino Teachers for Uruguay in The Philippine
     Star 13.6.2013
     Retrieved on 16.01.2019 from
     https://www.pressreader.com/@Paul_Woods.3

4   Retrieved on 17.01.2019 from
     https://lifestyle.inquirer.net/246209/finally-book-theater-
     pioneer-naty-crame-rogers/

5   Retrieved on 17.01.2019 from
     https://en.wikipedia.org/wiki/Lea_Salonga

6   Torres, E and Smith, M, L, 1990, English for Fisheries
     Technology, National Book Store

7   Retrieved on 17.01.2019 from
     https://www.diffordsguide.com/encyclopedia/372/bars/t he-
     most-bizarre-bar-hobbit-house-manila

8   Retrieved on 17.01.2019 from
     https://www.washingtonpost.com/news/worldviews/wp/
     2016/09/13/in-the-philippines-jim-turners-heartbroken-

hobbits-mourn-the-loss-of-their-
patron/?noredirect=on&utm_term=.e6d8ea17503e

9   Retrieved on 17.01.2019 from
        https://www.vigattintourism.com/tourism/articles/The-
        Great-Ancestral-Marcos-Mansion

10   Retrieved on 17.01.2019 from
        https://www.theguardian.com/commentisfree/2018/
        sep/29/satanic-verses-sowed-seeds-of-rift-grown-ever-wider

11   Retrieved on 17.01.2019 from
        http://www.gcf.org.ph/about/history

12   Retrieved on 18.01.2019 from
        https://en.wikipedia.org/wiki/1989_Philippine_coup_
        attempt

13   Retrieved on 22.01.2019 from
        https://en.wikipedia.org/wiki/Bras%C3%ADlia

14   Retrieved on 22.01.2019 from
        https://www.bbc.co.uk/news/magazine-20632277

15   ibid

16   ibid

17   People in the news. Article in *Past, Present Future* Number
        10, July 1993. Brasilia, British Council. p1

18   Woods, P. *English in Latin America* in *Concord* Issue 2
        May-November 1995, p6
        Retrieved on 22.01.2019 from
        http://eiflavioserique.blogspot.com/

19   Woods, *P Synergy: Improving the Circulation of Pedagogic
        and Cultural Energy* in LABCI News June-July 1994, p4.

20   Retrieved on 23.01.2019 from
        https://theculturetrip.com/south-america/brazil/articles/the-
        ultimate-guide-to-celebrating-2018-carnival-in-olinda-brazil/

21   Retrieved on 24.01.2019 from

https://www.facebook.com/groups/244794172632088/?t
nstr=*F&fref=gs&dti=244794172632088&hc_location
=group_dialog

22 Potter, M. *A Personal Word*, in Barbara L and Scott M (eds),
1994 Reflections on Language Learning, Multilingual
Matters.

23 The British Council 1985 Dunford Seminar Report
Language Skills in National Curriculum Development.

24 Woods, P. 1995. UKIPST Monitoring Report.   Unpublished
document, Manchester, Consultancy Group,Professional
Services, The British Council.

25 Tse Tso Y. W. 1997 *An Evaluation of the UK Immersion
Programme for Student Teachers (UKIPST)* Unpublished
research report, HKIEd, Hong Kong, quoted in Mok
M.M.C and Ching, C. et al, 2008, Subject Teaching and
Teacher Education in the New Century: Research and
Innovation, Dordrecht, HKIEd and Kluwer Academic
Publishers.

26 Woods, P. *African Jewel Chooses English Over French* in EL
Gazette December 1995 p3.

27 Retrieved on 2.02.2019 from
https://englishagenda.britishcouncil.org/global
-   projects/track-record/step-project-mozambique

28 ibid

29 Retrieved on 2.02.2019 from
https://dblackie.blogs.com/the_language_business/
2006/09/index.html

30 Retrieved on 2.02.2019 from
http://sheinspiresher.com/marta-tomazia-guimaraes
-   madeira-the-mozambican-with-moxie/

31 Retrieved on 2.02.2019 from
https://www.theguardian.com/uk/1999/nov/16/monarchy
comment

32   ibid

33   ibid

34   Retrieved on 4.02.2019 from
http://floodlist.com/africa/mozambique-floods-2000

35   Retrieved on 4.02.2019 from
http://news.bbc.co.uk/1/hi/world/africa/662472.stm

36   Retrieved on 4.02.2019 from
https://www.theguardian.com/world/2013/feb/14/chinese-
shark-fin-soup-mozambique

37   ibid

38   ibid

39   Retrieved on 6.2.2019 from
https://en.wikipedia.org/wiki/Grande_Hotel_Beira

40   Woods, P. *Far-reaching Value of Peacekeeping English* in
Network News, Issue 35 January 2002, London, The British
Council, p10.

41   ibid, p10

42   ibid, p10

43   Retrieved on 08.02.2019 from
https://en.wikipedia.org/wiki/Craig_Murray

44   Retrieved on 08.02.2019 from
https://www.thetimes.co.uk/article/focus-the-british-
ambassador-says-his-hosts-are-boiling-people-to-death-
meet-craig-murray-our-man-in-uzbekistan-and-probably-
the-worlds-most-undiplomatic-diplomat-djx2pts6zxj

45   Retrieved on 08.02.2019 from
https://www.theguardian.com/politics/2004/jul/15/
foreignpolicy.uk

46   Retrieved 08.02.2019 from
https://www.theguardian.com/politics/2003/oct/18/uk.

foreignpolicy

47   ibid

48   Retrieved on 08.02.2019 from
https://en.wikipedia.org/wiki/Craig_Murray

49   Retrieved on 08.02.2019 from
https://www.theguardian.com/politics/2004/jul/15/
foreignpolicy.uk

50   Retrieved on 22.03.2019 from
https://en.wikipedia.org/wiki/Craig_Murray

51   Woods, P. *Progress at the PEP Conference in Croydon* in
PEP Newsletter No 9 January 2003. London, The British
Council p2.

52   Retrieved on 22.03.2019 from
https://www.bbc.co.uk/news/world-europe-16614209

53   Tony Crocker, personal communication

54   Retrieved on 08.02.2019 from
https://en.wikipedia.org/wiki/Saparmurat_Niyazov#
Presidential_pardons

55   ibid

56   Retrieved on 08.02.2019 from
https://www.independent.co.uk/news/obituaries/saparmurat-
niyazov-429556.html

57   Retrieved on 08.03.2019 from
https://www.theguardian.com/education/2009/may/22/tefl-
colombia

58   Retrieved on 13.02.2019 from
https://www.theguardian.com/uk/2005/may/27/human
rights.society

59   Retrieved on 13.02.2019 from
https://www.theguardian.com/society/2005/jul/20/

youthjustice.law1

60   Retrieved on 13.02.2019 from
        https://www.telegraph.co.uk/news/uknews/1494475/Home-
        Office-fights-yob-curfew-court-defeat.html

61   Retrieved on 13.02.2019 from
        https://www.libertyhumanrights.org.uk/human-
        rights/fighting-discrimination/young-people/curfews

62   Retrieved on 15.02.2019 from
        https://www.telegraph.co.uk/news/1901656/OGC-unveils-
        new-logo-to-red-faces.html

63   Retrieved on 15.02.2019 from
        https://www.bbc.co.uk/news/world-south-asia- 14965598

64   Retrieved on 15.02.2019 from
        https://reliefweb.int/sites/reliefweb.int/files/resources/
        Global%20Terrorism%20Index%20Report%202014.pdf

65   Routledge, P. *Nineteen Days in April: Urban Protest and
        Democracy in Nepal*, in Urban Studies 47(6) 1279–1299,
        May 2010, p1279
        Retrieved on 15.02.2019 from
        http://contested-cities.net/wpcontent/uploads/2014/03/
        2010_US_Routledge_Nineteen-Days-in-April.pdf

66   ibid, p1290

67   ibid, p1291

68   Retrieved on 16.02.2019 from
        https://roomfordiplomacy.com/kathmandu-kakani/

69   Retrieved on 18.02.2019 from
        http://himalayanhash.run/#home

70   Retrieved in 18.02.2019 from
        https://www.nao.org.uk/wp- content/uploads/
        2008/06/0708625.pdf

71   Retrieved on 18.02.2019 from

https://www.vfsglobal.com/dha/southafrica/pdf/final-Immigration-Regulations-2014-1.pdf

72 Retrieved on 18.02.2019 from
http://www.sundaystandard.info/prince-harry-launch-reading-challenge-local-primary-school

73 Retrieved on 18.02.2019 from
https://www.dailymail.co.uk/home/moslive/article-1320263/Prince-William-Prince-Harry-tour-Africa- talk-candidly-Ben-Fogle.html

74 Retrieved on 18.02.2019 from
http://www.goal-mouth.org/goalmouth-2010

75 Retrieved on 18.02.2019 from
https://www.facebook.com/ukinbotswana/posts/mophato-dance-group-goalmouth-members-of-the-mophato-dance-group-tell-their-stor/136970133022352/

76 Retrieved on 18.02.2109 from
http://thestiltz.com/

77 Retrieved on 22.03.2019 from
https://www.cpexposed.com/

78 Retrieved on 22.02.2019 from
https://www.newstatesman.com/uk-politics/2009/10/oxford-universitywealth-school

79 Retrieved on 22.02.2019 from
https://www.britishcouncil.org/organisation/transparency/freedom-of-information/disclosure-log/foi201524

80 Retrieved on 20.02.2019 from
https://www.mirror.co.uk/news/uk-news/top-torys-windfalls-as-he-sharpens-axe-247707

81 Retrieved on 20.02.2019 from
https://www.theguardian.com/politics/2013/nov/08/jeremy-hunt-17m-hotcourses-sale-inflexion

82 Retrieved on 22.02.2019 from
https://www.bbc.co.uk/news/business-38638577

83   Retrieved on 22.02.2019 from
      https://www.britishcouncil.org/organisation/press/briti   sh-
      council-education-uk-website

84   Retrieved on 22.02.2019 from
      https://thepienews.com/news/idp-education-acquires-
      hotcourses-group/

85   Retrieved on 22.02.2109 from
      https://dblackie.blogs.com/the_language_business/2011/01
      /the-second-most-used-resource-after-google.html

86   Retrieved on 22.02.2019 from
      https://hat4uk.wordpress.com/2011/03/05/hunt-balls-3-how-
      jeremy-hunt-won-a-lucrative-7-year- contract-with-the-
      british-council/

87   IATEFL, 2012. 2011 Brighton Conference Selections. T.
      Pattison(ed.) IATEFL.

88   Retrieved on 22 03.2019 from
      https://www.theguardian.com/society/2011/jun/21/ehrc-
      accused-mismanaging-taxpayers-money

89   Newton, K. and J. (eds.) 2015 The Brethren Movement
      Worldwide: Key Information 2015, Lockerbie, Opal
      Trust. p14

90   Davies, M, 2008. Saving My Arse: A Story of Cancers,
      Colons and Singapore Noodles. Self-published.

91   Banegas, D.L. (2013): ELT through videoconferencing in
      primary schools in Uruguay: first steps, Innovation in
      Language Learning and Teaching,
      DOI:10.1080/17501229.2013.794803
      Retrieved on 08.03.2019 from
      https://www.tandfonline.com/doi/abs/
      10.1080/17501229.2013.794803

92   Retrieved on 23.03.2019 from
      https://www.theguardian.com/travel/2018/jul/08/fray-bentos-
      uruguay-not-just-a-meat-pie

PAUL WOODS

ABOUT THE AUTHOR

After a decade spent teaching English and training primary school teachers in Nigeria, Brunei, Tanzania and Sierra Leone, Paul Woods finally achieved what had been his original ambition on leaving university – to join the British Council and enter the world of cultural diplomacy. The next three decades took him on a roller coaster ride on long-term assignments to eight countries and short-term visits to many more. Through letters, emails and often amusing anecdotes we get a glimpse of the trials and tribulations as well as the triumphs and joys of life as a cultural diplomat representing Britain, promoting the English language and helping to develop intercultural understanding around the world.

Printed in Great Britain
by Amazon

15867035R00132